D0806346

LOVE MATTERS

DENNIS LEONARD

Unless otherwise indicated, Scripture quotations are taken from the *New King James Version* of the Bible. Copyright © 1979, 1980, 1982 by Thomas Nelson, Inc. Used by permission. All rights reserved.

Scripture quotations marked KJV are taken from the *King James Version* of the Bible

Scripture quotations marked THE MESSAGE are from *The Message* by Eugene H. Peterson, copyright (c) 1993, 1994, 1995, 1996, 2000, 2001, 2002. Used by permission of NavPress Publishing Group. All rights reserved.

Scripture quotations marked AMP are taken from *The Amplified Bible*, Copyright © 1954, 1958, 1962, 1964, 1965, 1987 by the Lockman Foundation. Used by permission.

Scripture quotations marked NASB are taken from the *New American Standard Bible*. Copyright © 1960, 1962, 1963, 1968, 1971, 1972, 1973, 1975, 1977, 1995 by The Lockman Foundation. Used by permission. www.Lockman.org

Scripture quotations marked NIV are taken from the *Holy Bible, New International Version® NIV®*. Copyright © 1973, 1978, 1984, by International Bible Society. Used by permission of Zondervan. All rights reserved.

Scripture quotations marked NLT are taken from *The Holy Bible, New Living Translation*, copyright ©1996. Used by permission of Tyndale House Publishers, Inc., Wheaton, Illinois, 60189. All rights reserved.

Scripture quotations marked ESV are taken from *The Holy Bible, English Standard Version*, copyright ©2001 by Crossway Bibles, a division of Good News Publishers. Used by permission. All rights reserved.

Printed in the United States of America. All rights reserved under International Copyright Law. Contents and/or cover may not be reproduced in whole or in part in any form without the express written consent of the publisher.

Library of Congress Cataloging-in-Publication data pending
Leonard, Dennis
LOVE MATTERS
ISBN 1-880809-70-2

Copyright © 2007 by Legacy Publishers International

1301 South Clinton Street
Denver, Colorado 80247
phone: 303-283-7480
fax: 303-283-7536
www.legacypublishersinternational.com

Printed in the United States of America

15 14 13 12 11 10 09 08 07   1 2 3 4 5 6 7 8 9 10 11 12

Table of Contents

❧

CHAPTER ONE

God's Formula For Love

> "'Love the Lord your God with all your heart and with all your soul and with all your mind.' This is the first and greatest commandment. And the second is like it: 'Love your neighbor as yourself.'"
>
> MATTHEW 22:37-39 **NIV**

Many of us think we already know how to love. We think it's the rest of the world that needs to learn a thing or two about walking in love. But if we really knew anything at all about how to operate in the power of God's love, we wouldn't have the problems we have. If we really knew how to tap into the love of God, we wouldn't say the things we do; we wouldn't get upset when someone is a little rude; we wouldn't worry about people taking advantage of us. If we really knew how to love, our lives would be much different. Love will change us. Love will turn our lives around completely—and the lives of the people around us. It's amazing what can happen if we learn how to love with a God-kind of love.

Civilization has attempted to define love down through the ages. The Greeks used a variety of words to portray the many different aspects of love. In English, the definition of love is often limited to descriptions of physical affection or intense attraction for another person. The dictionary describes love as having to do with emotion. But as Christians we know that most of those things are nothing more than biochemical reactions, like the appetites that cause us to desire food or comfort.

As Christians we know that love is infinitely more than just a product of our desires. It's more than butterflies in our stomach when we have a crush, or hugging a friend that we are happy to see. Christian love is not a feeling we may or may not happen to have. Love is what we choose to do when our feelings tell us to do the exact opposite. Love is intentional—it's a deliberate decision. Godly love is a practice that requires discipline.

Love is intentional— it's a deliberate decision.

The truth is that love has very little to do with how we are feeling on the inside. Love is simply a decision we make about how to think, speak, and behave. Deciding to walk in love is not much different than deciding to get underneath an umbrella when it begins to rain. If I see it cloud over, I'll be mindful of my umbrella—and if it starts to sprinkle, I might get it out and open it. As soon as it really begins to pour, I'm all the way under it.

When I see a relational situation begin to grow a little overcast, I'll take hold of my love—and when things get stormy, I'll crawl right under God's covering of mercy. It protects me from getting soaked by offenses. When I choose to hang out under God's love, I am required to change some things I might otherwise say or do. If I crawl under the umbrella of love—meaning that I make a decision to love you no matter what you do or say to me—then I am in a place where I can operate in the *God-kind* of love. I simply have to decide to get under that umbrella.

Love Is a Choice

God gave us the formula for how to walk in His love. It's not rocket science. It's as simple as this, we are to love the Lord our God with all of our hearts, and we are to love our neighbors as ourselves. Two simple commandments: Love God. Love people. If I'm going to love people, I've got to forgive people that I don't want to forgive. That means I have to let go of the issues that I don't want to let go of. I have to make a deliberate choice to treat people differently than how I *want to* treat them. While our natural man—our sin nature—is critical, unforgiving, and unkind, our spirit-man—the part of us renewed by the Spirit of Christ—is sympathetic, merciful, and loving.

If we really want to be like Christ—which is what defines us as Christians—then we must love people no matter how unlovable they seem. In other words, we must make a quality decision to walk in love at all times—with *all* people. We must choose to get under the umbrella of love, and stay under that love cover no matter what goes on around us.

One of the keys to being like our Lord is not to be critical. Unfortunately, Christians are some of the most critical people in the world, often in the name of Christ! Even Jesus said He did not come into the world to condemn it, but to save it! (see Jn. 3:17) At the most crucial hour in world history, when our Master hung on the cross, He said, "Father, forgive them; for they know not what they do" (Lk. 23:34, KJV). Has there ever been a time in your life when "they" were crucifying you, and you said, "Lord, just forgive them. They don't even know what they're do-ing?" Or did you want to punch them in the nose and then repent later?

I'm sure you will agree that finding fault with other people is one of the easiest things to do! Yet if we choose to walk in God's mercy, in His Spirit of love and forgiveness, we will find ourselves becoming more and more uncomfort-able with criticizing others. The more we grow in Christ, the less "natural" it will become for us to slip into our old pattern of faultfinding.

Love: The Key to Your Success

Your success in life will be measured by how you treat others. The way you measure out love to others is the way it will be measured back to you. What you sow in the lives of others is what will grow in your own life. Paul tells us to "put on a heart of compassion" (Col. 3:12, NASB), just like putting on a coat. Sometimes you don't want to wear that coat, but if it's cold outside, you will have to put it on. Many times you have to slip on a coat of love when you really don't want to. It is a coat of kindness, compassion, and forgiveness. In other words, you don't have to *feel* loving to love. It's something that you choose to do by faith.

Faith prevails when love prevails.

Your mind says, "If you forgive them, they'll turn right around and do it to you again. Don't let them treat you like that!" In truth, God is saying, "If you'll have enough faith to love them anyway, I'll make it up to you before it's over." Our flesh says, "Get even." God says, "If you'll let it go, I'll make it up to you." That takes faith, and faith works by love. It takes a profound love of God to let things go for His Name's sake, and without that love our faith will not succeed. Faith prevails when love prevails.

The truth is, there is no love in judgmental attitudes. Anyone who is judgmental does not know how to love. Whenever we find fault with or criticize one another, all we do is prove that we don't know how to love, regardless of what we say. Jesus said, "Judge not, lest you bring judgment upon yourself" (Mt. 7:1, paraphrased). Any time we judge one another; any time we are harsh; any time we gossip, criticize, or find fault with one another, we give the enemy an opportunity to divide and conquer in our relationships.

For the first ten years of my ministry I had a sign on my desk and on my mirror that said, "Encourage others." I needed that constant reminder because it was not my nature to be encouraging. Having been raised in a household that was very critical resulted in my being critical when I grew up. Because of the environment I grew up in and became accustomed to, I became a master of criticism. That is why I had to make a conscious, daily decision to change. It was hard work, as hard, in its own way, as physical exercise, but with the Lord's help I have been able to overcome my critical habits. For many of us, this one area will be the most challenging in learning to put on the new man and really growing up in Christ. However, the end result is worth every bit of effort we put onto it, because cultivating the habit of love leads to increased favor and greater success.

The Power of Life and Death

One of the keys to walking in love is to resist saying anything unkind about someone else. If we're going to be in God's will, we have to guard the words we speak. Solomon said, "Death and life are in the power of the tongue" (Prov. 18:21a). If you are going to grow up in Christ, you will have to get a handle on what comes out of your mouth.

Your words have the power to change someone's life. Parents, you have the ability to change the direction of your children's lives by the words you speak not only to them, but also about them. Husbands and wives, your words can heal or hinder your spouse, whether spoken in or out of his or her presence.

If you are someone who speaks negatively about people, or who simply spreads information about someone else, you are a gossiper. People who gossip do not really know how to love. But you can change someone's life by encouraging and "loving on" that person—and that means not discussing his or her shortcomings with other people. Jesus said, "It's not what enters a man's mouth that defiles him, but what comes out of his mouth" (Mk. 7:15, paraphrased).

Being negative or critical of other people will also bring unhappiness into your own life. Your life follows your words. When you get your words turned around, your whole life will turn around. Peter tells us that if we want to enjoy life, and if we want to see good days in our lives, we must stop being critical and stop talking negatively about other people (see 1 Pet. 3:10). People will never measure up to all of our expectations. Most of us don't even realize how negative we are every day. We tend to be unkind and don't even realize it because it is our sin nature. Even though as Christians we are crucified with Christ, every once in awhile the critical, dead man rises up out of that coffin! The important thing is that we recognize it and are quick to repent.

Spiritual growth is a process. Learning to walk in love is a lifelong process; as soon as we overcome a challenge in one area, another will rise up to test and stretch us. Because God's love is infinite, the lessons of love we must learn are endless!

More Love Requires More of God

Walking in love is a decision. When I choose to get under this umbrella of love, when I make the decision to love people I don't want to love, what I'm really saying is, "God, I want Your will in my life; Lord, not my will, but Your will be done." If I choose to talk about someone's failures, then I am not doing the Lord's will, but my own. There is no love in gossip. Gossip is about trying to bring somebody down. It is about exposing someone's failure right at the point where God said, "Love covers a multitude of sins" (1 Pet. 4:8).

The Bible tells us that love believes the best. We read in 1 Corinthians 13:7 that love bears all things—love hopes all things—love endures all things. If you know how to love, people will be drawn to you. No matter how young or old you are, or whether you're single or married, if you know how to love, you will attract people like a magnet. If people are not drawn to

12

you, it is because you do not know how to love. We need God to teach us how to love, because we humans, in the natural, cannot love and forgive the way God wants us to love and forgive. That's why Jesus said, "I am the vine, you are the branches" (John 15:5). The closer we get to Him, the more we will draw strength from Him, and the more we will know how to love.

> ### *If you want to know how to love, you must get closer to God. The closer you get to Him, the greater your capacity to love.*

First John 4:8 tells us that God *is* love. If you want to know how to love, you must get closer to God. The closer you get to Him, the greater your capacity to love. There is only one way that you can love people who have caused great pain in your life, and that's if you connect to the Giver of love—the God of love. If you're not intimately connected to the Lord—*in love* with Jesus—you won't be able to *give love*. You can't give what you don't have. Only He can empower you to love with the kind of love that sets people free. That's a primary reason we attend church—to learn how to love, give, and live selflessly. This is what liberates and draws people to God. The closer we draw to the Lord, the more we tap into the Source of love, and the more life we find we have to give.

It is no secret that God's love releases rivers of life into a parched world. Not only does love cover a multitude of sins with waves of mercy and grace; our faith can only work in an environment of love. Perhaps the reason you haven't received your miracle is because of your love walk. If you'll decide to walk under that umbrella of love—if you will make that deliberate decision—your whole life will change. Pray that the Lord expands your capacity to love, and that the Holy Spirit leads you into a deeper knowledge of love. Ask God to teach you how to operate in the miracle-working, life-giving power of *His* love.

CHAPTER TWO

What It Really Means to Love

Love

> Love is patient, love is kind. It does not envy, it does not boast, it is not proud. It is not rude, it is not self-seeking, it is not easily angered, it keeps no record of wrongs. Love does not delight in evil but rejoices with the truth. It always protects, always trusts, always hopes, always perseveres.
>
> Love never fails. But where there are prophecies, they will cease; where there are tongues, they will be stilled; where there is knowledge, it will pass away.
>
> And now these three remain: faith, hope and love. But the greatest of these is love.
>
> 1 CORINTHIANS 13:4-8, 13 NIV

Many people, especially Christians, think there's not much they can learn about love. They know how to give love, and they know how to receive love—but human love is not at all like the God-kind of love.

Let me ask you this, what would you say is the meaning of life?

Would you say the meaning of life is to be happy? Would you say it's to be successful? Would you say it's to be comfortable? How you answer this question determines how you choose to live your life. If you say the meaning of life is to have fun, then you probably have a lot of fun in your life. If that's what you think life is about, that's just what you do.

Perhaps you would say that the meaning of life is to be comfortable. In that case, you are probably planning your next home improvement project, or vacation, or possibly anticipating retirement. If you believe the meaning of life is to love those around you, then you will go to extra lengths to love others. The meaning you place on life defines your core beliefs and values, and all of these together determine your behavior.

But if you say the meaning of life is to love God with all of your heart, and to love others as you love yourself, then you will begin to live a supernatural life. You will be like Paul the apostle: Eternity-minded and crying out to God, "Here's my life. I surrender it all to You. Not my will, but Your will be done."

Making Your Life Count

In 1 Corinthians 13:4-8, Paul tells us that without love, everything we say or do is without meaning. All loveless efforts are empty, no matter how great they might seem. He said we can speak with the tongues of angels, but if we don't know how to love, our words are empty. The power of our words is determined by the love our words carry. If you're having trouble in a relationship, the first question you should ask yourself is, "Am I communicating love? Am I speaking to others in the spirit of love?" No matter what words you use, if your speech is not backed up by genuine love, your words are empty. If your words are angry, spiteful, or critical, you will continue to have trouble in your home and in all your relationships.

Paul says that even if you have the faith to move mountains, but don't have love, it's not going to amount to a thing. You can believe you are a prophet of God, but if you don't have love, you are nothing. You can say you believe in Jesus, go to church every Sunday, sing in the choir, and give to the building fund, but if you don't have love, you haven't accomplished anything.

What you believe means nothing unless you are demonstrating love in your life.

Interestingly, lots of people say they believe in God, but very few know anything about the love of God. What you believe means nothing unless you are demonstrating love in your life. Christianity is not so much about rules as it is about a lifestyle. It's about a walk of faith. When you forgive someone who has hurt you, what you are really doing is walking by faith. You are saying, "Okay, you hurt me, but God told me to forgive you, so I'm going to let it go. I'm going to believe that somehow by letting it go, God will make it work for the best of all." That's faith in action.

The Christian walk is a walk of faith. The Christian is not somebody who just says, "I believe." Christians are people who demonstrate their faith by acting out their love for others. Jesus said that non-Christians would know Christians by their love—not by our denomination or by how often we go to church. He said they would know us by the way we set aside our differences, by the way we help one another, by the way we bear one another's burdens; in short, by the way we love one another.

Without love, everything we give or accomplish is in vain. You could conquer the world for Christ, but unless you had the love of God motivating you, it wouldn't mean anything. You could give your life for the sake of the gospel, traveling all over the world, but if you didn't have love in your heart, it would amount to nothing. You could have the faith of a great miracle worker, but without love, it wouldn't count for anything. You could speak with the eloquence of a great orator, but if love was not your primary inspiration, you still would miss the true meaning of life.

Love's Proof

The Bible says that God measures our love for Him by the way we love other people. Specifically, it says that if we do not love our brother, we cannot truly call ourselves Christian (see 1 Jn. 4:20.) This has nothing to do with being "right"; it has to do with obeying God. Any time we choose not to forgive someone, we are turning our back on God. Any time we walk around with a chip on our shoulder, complaining about how someone has treated us, we are in disobedience to the Lord. If we are loving and serving God, we are going to get hurt (see Jn. 15:18-20.) That's just the way the world is. But as we grow up in Christ, we learn not to live by feelings, but according to the Word of God.

It's not easy to love people who have hurt you, but you can do it because God's love is shed abroad in your heart (see Rom. 5:5). You can be angry in your head, but still pursue love in your heart. You can be hurt in your heart but still operate out of love. When you are hurting and wounded, you can still put your arm around somebody and say, "How are you today?" That's the love of God at work in you. That's spiritual maturity. God's love will cause you to do things you don't feel like doing.

When you were a child, you just wanted to eat sweet things. When you grew up, you understood that you had to eat vegetables too to stay healthy. Spiritual maturity is a little like that. It is doing what you need to do rather than only what you want to do. It is disciplining yourself to obey God instead of your flesh—choosing to follow God instead of your natural desires.

Your Love Account

We prove our love for the Lord when we love people who don't deserve our love. One day, when we stand before God, we will be asked to give an account of our lives. We will all be accountable as to whether or not we loved God's people.

So what does it mean to love? You might say, "I love lattés," or, "I love chocolate." You might love your car, or the ocean, or your dog. The real question is, what does it truly mean to love? The dictionary says that love is an emotion or feeling. Scripture, on the other hand, says that love has nothing to do with emotions or feelings. Love is just the opposite; it is denying our feelings and emotions, and obeying God. It is choosing to love those who spitefully use us, who persecute us, and who call themselves our enemies (see Mt. 5:44.).

> *True love—godly love—always gives,*
> *nourishes, and serves.*

Most people really don't know the first thing about love. In their minds, love is for those who meet their needs, or who seem outwardly loveable, or who are simply lovely to look at.

That is a very self-centered love, not genuine love. Selfish love leads to jealousy, envy, and strife. Once someone stops meeting your needs, you become at odds with them, and they are of no further use to you. Self-centered love pulls and takes for itself. It depletes and never gives anything back, which is why it cannot truly be called love. True love—godly love—*always* gives, nourishes, and serves.

Where there is worldly love, people will begin to criticize those who stop meeting their needs for adoration or comfort. They will act negatively toward those who threaten them in some way, because there is jealousy or envy in their heart. That kind of heart is not alive to God. A heart alive to God is grounded in love—a love that acts in faith. Love is more than saying something; it is doing something. It's more than feelings. It's more than sentimental jargon. Love is made alive in action, because, just like faith, love without works is dead.

When I first started going out with my wife, I bought her stuff all the time. Every time I found a shoe store, I would buy her a pair of shoes. I still do the same thing. Why? Because love gives. Love can't help but give; giving is the nature of love. If we loved people the way God does, we would be consumed by thoughts of how we could give to them in meaningful ways and be a blessing even to those who might not know the first thing about love.

Love in Action

Real love is about action. Real love gets you up in the middle of the night to care for your sick child, while gladly wishing you could take your child's fear or fever upon yourself. While natural love takes care of a sick friend, God's love takes care of a sick stranger. Perhaps the greatest example of this in the New Testament is Jesus' story of the Good Samaritan (see Lk. 10:30-37). In fact, Jesus used this very story to illustrate what it means to love God with all our heart, and our neighbor as ourselves.

Natural love compels you to be patient with your spouse when he or she is grumpy, or to remain faithful when you are tempted to stray—but God's love goes further. God's love looks always to give what is needed rather than what is deserved. Living godly love means treating others the way God treats you. Jesus said, "Do to others as you would have them do to you" (Lk. 6:31, NIV). Would you really want God to treat you the way you seflishly treat others?

Godly love is about loving others the way God loves you. It's forgiving others the way God forgives you. God's love serves. Genuine love will reveal itself when you take on the heart of a servant and serve someone who doesn't deserve it.

Jesus was the greatest servant of all. He was the King of all glory, yet He came to this earth and didn't expect people to wait on Him. Instead, He waited on them. He had the heart of a servant. The anointing came on Jesus as He served. Likewise, if you'll find a place to serve in your church, the anointing of God will touch your life. It's not about how much information you can get in church—because the more knowledge you get without putting it to use, the more arrogant you will become—but about using your life to serve.

When you start serving, everything seems to improve. Why? Because you get the focus off of you and your problems and start living for a greater purpose. As you begin to humbly serve, many doors will open for God to speak to you and bless you. Jesus teaches that whatever we do for the least of folks, we're doing for Him, and that those who serve Him in this manner will "inherit the kingdom prepared for [them] from the foundation of the world" (Mt. 25:34; see verses 34-46.)

As you begin to use your life to give to others, what you give will come back to you in a magnificent way.

We live in a day when people don't want to serve. They want to know what's in it for them. Most people are more interested in what they can get than in what they can give. Jesus said, "It is more blessed to give than to receive" (Acts 20:35b).

You will profit more by giving than you ever will by receiving. Jesus said, "Give, and it shall be given unto you; good measure, pressed down, and shaken together, and running over" (Luke 6:38, KJV). He meant that as you begin to use your life to give to others, what you give will come back to you in a magnificent way.

Losing Your Life

God has given each of us certain gifts and talents. He didn't give them to us just so we could make a bunch of money for ourselves and then die and leave it to our children. His purpose in giving us gifts and talents is so that we can be a blessing to others by giving to them as He has given to us. You will never fully grasp the meaning of life until you learn to be a giver.

Once you gave your life to Christ, your life became His. It's no longer your own. Life is no longer all about you. As long as you keep the mindset that your life is about you, you will continually miss out on all that God has for you. Your heart will grow hard and you will become blind to His direction.

You walk out your love for God by serving and loving people.

So how do you really *give* your life to the Lord? How do you go about laying it down? It's simple - by loving others and by serving them. Just jump in and let God use you. The answer is simple, but it is not automatic. You have to make up your mind to find a way to serve God's people. Find a need and fill it. There is never a shortage of needs to be met in the church— or out in the world. Look around your community. You walk out your love for God by serving and loving people.

When you get your focus off of yourself, the world around you will change. Whatever your need is, whatever your issues are, if you will get the focus off of you and begin to serve and love the people around you, somehow everything has a way of working out. That's God's economy.

Love Commits

God's love never quits. The love of God is faithful, loyal, and steadfast. God's love endures to the end and never fails. When you understand that love is not a feeling, you can always choose to love instead of being swept away by whatever you feel.

When you choose to love someone, you take on a great responsibility. No longer can you do whatever you want without regard for those closest to you. You are accountable to the ones you love. In the professional world, you must take responsibility and be accountable for your actions, good or bad, successful or unsuccessful. Being professional is a lot like walking in love. If you would conduct yourself in such a manner on the job—choose to behave toward others in a certain way because it is a requirement in the workplace—how much more should you choose to treat the same way those you are in a covenant relationship with, such as your spouse or your brothers and sisters in Christ?

Real love is committed and accountable. That is how we are to love one another in our homes and in the church. When you say, "I don't believe in making a financial commitment to the youth center, or a time commitment to the Sunday school," be careful that you are not caught up in loving yourself more than you do God's people.

Our commitments show what we truly love.

People will make a commitment for a boat, or a car, or a timeshare, but won't make a commitment for the kingdom of God. We need to be sure to check the motives governing our lives. Our commitments show what we truly love. How I spend my time, treasure, and talents shows where my heart is (see Matthew 6:21). I say it this way, "Show me your checkbook, and I'll show you what you love."

Sacrificial Love

Don't be afraid to make a commitment. Don't be fearful of committing to a marriage or a ministry. Real love is all about commitment—it is a love that is not afraid. First John 4:18-19 says, "There is no fear in love; but perfect love casts out fear, because fear involves torment. But he who fears has not been made perfect in love. We love Him because He first loved us." Make the sacrifice and be the first to show love. Love is irresistible. If you want a love response, then you must proactively love. We love God because He first loved us. A situation or a relationship might require you to make the first loving move. And because you first showed love, love will be the result.

We show God we love Him by making loving sacrifices for Him. You can give without loving, but you cannot love without giving. Real love makes sacrifices. There is no sacrifice I wouldn't make for my wife or my children. When you sacrifice, it is for the greater purpose of somebody else. When you find your greater purpose, it's not so much about you as it is about how God wants to use you to touch and bless other people's lives.

God already knows what your needs are, but He wants you to learn to give sacrificially so that He can supernaturally bless you. Sacrifice isn't natural. Self-sacrifice is in itself a supernatural act. Sacrificial giving is a spiritual test for all of us, but God blesses us as we give of ourselves. Every time you make a loving sacrifice, you become more like Jesus. He hung on the cross and died in our place because of His great love for us. Whenever you make a sacrifice, whatever it is, you are becoming more Christ-like.

Start giving, start serving, and start loving in a whole new way. If you learn what Christian love really means—and put it into practice—you will see your life and the world around you change.

The sign of a Christian is not a cross around the neck—entertainers, rappers, and drug dealers wear crosses. No, the true sign of a Christian is not wearing a cross, but *bearing* a cross; picking up the cross of Christ daily in self-giving love. A Christian is someone who has made a decision to put God first and to love with the God-kind of love.

CHAPTER THREE

Growing Up in Love

When I was a child, I talked like a child, I thought
like a child, I reasoned like a child; now that I have
become a man, I am done with childish ways and have
put them aside.

And so faith, hope, love abide...these three; but the
greatest of these is love.

1 Corinthians 13:11, 13 AMP

For many of us, childhood was a time of simple pleasures.
We occupied ourselves with having fun, hanging out with
friends, dreaming about the future, and being spoiled by our
grandparents. As children, we lived carefree lives. Our biggest
concerns may have been who we would play with at recess,
what we were going to get for Christmas, or how we would
celebrate our birthday. Relatively speaking, childhood was a
time of exploring and fulfilling our heart's desires. Little was
expected of us and much was given.

As we grow up, we learn that life is not always all about
us. We begin by learning how to share, and then how to give,

29

and finally how to forgive. By the time we reach adulthood, we have learned, hopefully, to be generous and gracious. We might be a little less selfish, at least in obvious ways, but at our core we are still very self-seeking. That's how our sin nature is. Our pride seems to grow as we do and becomes more refined in many ways; so refined, in fact, that often we don't even call it pride anymore. We might call it dignity or self-assurance, but whatever name we give it, in truth it is really just another form of self-centeredness in a more sophisticated package. It takes the Spirit of truth to reveal these areas to us and help us trade in our childish ways for true spiritual maturity.

Understanding Spiritual Maturity

Although we need the help of the Holy Spirit to mature spiritually, maturity is not about how long we pray in the Holy Ghost or how often we prophesy. Growing up spiritually is about walking in love even when our circumstances shout against it. Someone cuts you off in traffic or speaks badly about you at work, yet you keep your cool and respond with grace rather than with harsh words or gestures. That is a sign of spiritual maturity. You will know you are maturing in the Lord when your mother-in-law doesn't get under your skin anymore. When you are able to love people who are unloving, or just plain unlovely, then you'll know the Spirit is at work in you.

We have made spiritual maturity into some lofty concept, elevating it in our minds to something attainable only by pious monks, devout scholars, great mystical gurus, or masters of spiritual warfare. No matter how great any of these people may seem, however, they are nothing without love. Too many of them have not succeeded at achieving the one thing required of true greatness in the sight of God—selfless love. Spiritual maturity can be defined by the degree to which one is able to love selflessly.

> ### Spiritual maturity can be defined by the degree to which one is able to love selflessly.

I heard a story of a monk who traveled the world looking for enlightenment. He journeyed on foot, carried nothing with him, and quietly begged for food and shelter wherever he went. His disciplines were silence, suffering, and solitude. Soon his humble state of affairs became a way of life that others admired and emulated. Disciples followed him on his journey, seeking to learn a "higher way." The monk was given a monastery atop a mountain, from where he could meditate day and night. He taught others to give up all their worldly belongings and to wander the streets, begging for their daily needs.

Dying to self was the path to enlightenment and became the ultimate goal of the monk's followers. The local town became inundated with starving and sick "seekers of enlightenment," and had to set up shelters and clinics to care for the homeless. Christian relief agencies were called in to minister to those "seekers" in need who had placed such a burden on the community because they had so successfully "died to self." Sometimes there is nothing more selfish or proud than withdrawing from the world for your own sense of enlightenment. Where is the love in pursuing vows of poverty, silence, and solitude? Christ did not come so that we could suffer in silence, but so we could loudly rejoice and share an increasingly abundant life with everyone around us.

True spiritual warfare is simply walking in love when we don't want to walk in love.

Once we understand spiritual maturity, we can begin to understand what is involved in spiritual warfare. Most folks understand that effective engagement in spiritual warfare requires some degree of spiritual maturity, but they do not understand why. True spiritual warfare is simply walking in love when we don't want to walk in love. Spiritual warfare has more to do with overcoming the selfishness of our flesh than with battling demons. It is a love war.

The enemy of our souls understands that if he can keep us out of love, he can keep us off the path of life. But it is our own sin nature that fights to remain childish, and our childish self strives to protect itself through fear and pride. Our enemy is already bound and under our feet, so our job is to renew our minds and discipline our flesh with the power and love of God. We must perfect our love in order to have victory over our enemies—both spiritual *and* natural.

While we might think that binding the devil is spiritual, the most spiritual thing we can do is walk in love when our flesh is telling us to do just the opposite. Paul said that prophesying is good, seeing into the future is good, and the gifts of the Spirit are good, but that none of them are any good at all if we don't walk in love. We'll never know true spiritual maturity until we make a decision to forgive people that we don't want to forgive. We'll never grow up in Christ spiritually until we put on a heart of love. It is one thing to call ourselves by the name "Christian"—which means literally, "little Christ"—but it is something else entirely to mature into the kind of person that name truly fits. My brothers and sisters, it is time for us to grow up as Christians, and this means learning to love as Jesus loves.

Lord, Teach Me to Love You

Many of us assume that because we are Christians, we know how to love. We think we know all about love because we think we know all about God. Yes, we know the Bible tells us that God is love (see 1 Jn. 4:8). We also know that God's love is shed abroad in our hearts when we accept Jesus as our Lord and Savior (see Rom. 5:5). But how can we know the first thing about love if we give our spouse the silent treatment for two days? We don't have a clue how to love. If we can't love—as in being loving toward—the people who love us, how are we going to love—as in being loving toward—our enemies? John said that if we hate our brother and say we love God, we are liars. Worse yet, if we're not able to love those we can see, how can we love Him Whom we can't see? (1 Jn. 4:20.)

If God loved us even when we didn't deserve it, what right do we have to withhold love from others just because we think they are "unworthy"?

Godly love is unconditional love; it does not depend on merit, but is extended freely to all, even those who don't deserve it. Come to think of it, none of us deserve love, especially the love of God. Our sin nature disqualifies us. Fortunately for us, God doesn't look at it that way. We don't deserve His love, yet He loves us anyway. And that's the way He wants us to be as His children.

The genuineness of our faith is measured by the genuineness of our love, not only for God, but also for others. If God loved us even when we didn't deserve it, what right do we have to withhold love from others just because we think they are "unworthy"? What if they *are* unworthy? So what? So are we. And yet, this limited, "conditional" love is the kind that many of us most often give and receive. Here's what we say (in attitude and behavior, if not in words), "If you treat me the way I want you to treat me, and if you do what I want you to do, then I will love you. But if not, then I won't even talk to you." Or, "I love you when you're good, but not when you're bad." Have you ever heard that one?

It's all a faith issue, believing that even if someone doesn't love us, as long as we show God we have faith in Him, somehow He will work things out on our lives. Jesus gave us the secret to successful living when He said, "Love your enemies. Do good to those who hate you. Bless those who curse you" (Mt. 5:44, paraphrased). Yet, if some guy flips us off in traffic, we're ready to run him off the road! Jesus told us to bless those who curse us, and pray for those who mistreat us. Why would He command such a thing? Because He knew that we cannot hate somebody we're praying for. It is a love test.

Whether we like it or not, we must live by every word that proceeds out of the mouth of God. We can't go by feelings. If we go by feelings, we'll never tithe. If we go by feelings, we'll always get offended. If we go by feelings, we'll never love people who hurt us. It's a love test. Someone may have offended you, but now you have a chance to pass the love test. You may have been hurt by a friend's betrayal, but now you have a chance to submit your hurt to the love test. If you still get an attitude when people don't do what you want them to do, then God still has a work to do inside of you. If you've been to church and learned the Word of God, yet the bitterness in your heart toward somebody on your job remains, God wants you to know that nothing is going to work out in your life until you pass the love test.

If a certain person walking into the room causes you to get an attitude, then you have not passed the love test. If just thinking about a particular person makes your blood boil, God can't do anything for you because you haven't passed the love test. We think we know how to love, but if we can't be loving toward even our own family members when they hurt us, how are we going to love our enemies?

Fervent Love

Peter said, "Above all, keep fervent in your love for one another, because love covers a multitude of sins" (1 Pet. 4:8 NASB). Have you ever noticed how church folks sometimes can get on your nerves? In fact, some of them will get on your last nerve! But so will many of the people you encounter in the world. That's just the way human nature is. This is why Peter says we must "keep fervent" in our love for each other. I think the Amplified Bible really captures the force of what Peter is saying here, "Above all things have intense and unfailing love for one another, for love covers a multitude of sins—forgives and disregards the offenses of others" (1 Pet. 4:8 AMP).

We are to maintain an "intense and unfailing love" that "forgives and disregards the offenses of others." This means that whenever we discover that someone has failed, we don't repeat it to anyone. Instead, as true and serious followers of Christ, we *cover* it. Love protects. Love defends. Love does not expose other people's faults. Love does not gossip. Christians are notorious for concealing gossip under a cloak of false piety, "Oh, could we just pray over Sister Johnson, because, you know, she's been sleeping with Leroy. I'm not gossiping, I just think we ought to hold her up in prayer!" This too is a love test. Do we love our brothers and sisters in Christ enough not to broadcast their flaws and failures before others?

Do we love our brothers and sisters in Christ enough not to broadcast their flaws and failures before others?

"Above all, keep fervent in your love for one another." When we walk in love, we don't condemn people when they fail. We all fail at one time or another and we are never more vulnerable than when we have just experienced failure. The last thing we need is for someone to rub it in or to announce our failure to the world. So here's the love test: When someone you love fails, do you expose that failure for all to see, or do you try to protect and support that loved one in spite of the failure? Just as God's love covers our sin, when we love one another with the God-kind of love, we will cover each other in our failures.

Love is the key factor that identifies us as children of God. What was it Jesus said? Did Jesus say people would know us by our denomination? Did He say they would know us by the size of our buildings? No. He said they would know us by our love (see Jn. 13:35). We can tell people all day long, "I love you, I love you, I love you," but it means nothing if we don't back it up with action. Talk is cheap. But putting on a heart of love and loving somebody who is not lovable always carries a cost, at least in a little effort.

Don't tell me you love God if you hate your ex-wife. Don't tell me you love God if you hate a race of people. Don't tell me you love God if you hate your boss. Paul prayed that there would be no divisions among us. Division is evidence of lack of love. Christianity is supposed to be about kindness; it's supposed to be about love; it's supposed to be about not being judgmental. This may sound simple, but if you can learn the secret of the God-kind of love, you will be a spiritual hero, because love is the most powerful weapon you have for dealing with your enemies.

The Transforming Power of Love

As Christians, we have the power to change people's lives through love. When we reach out through ministries to un-wed mothers, we are saying, "We love you." When we start a youth ranch, we are saying to all those abused kids and those that are up for adoption, "We love you." When we reach out in the name of Christ to those in prison, we are saying, "We love you." When we reach out to the hungry through a food ministry, we are saying, "We love you." Paul said that love never fails. The truth is people cannot resist genuine love. This is true for all of us. In fact, we'll make fools out of ourselves to be loved. We'll go places we shouldn't go. We'll spend money we shouldn't spend. We'll talk on the phone to people we should never be talking to.

I can't begin to count the number of people I've laid hands on for healing, where, as I prayed for them, God spoke to me on the inside and told me just to put my arms around them and love them, because they needed love right then more than they needed anything else. Love will heal when nothing else can. Perhaps that's why all the biblical commandments are based on loving God and loving our fellow man. If we look at the Ten Commandments, we see that the first four have to do with loving God, while the remaining six deal with loving people. Love is all about how we respect God by how we treat other people. God knows that as long as we're more concerned about ourselves than we are about others, we will never walk in true victory.

Love will heal when nothing else can.

Jesus said that we are supposed to lose our life for His sake in order to find it (see Mt. 16:25). We are supposed to give in order to be given back to in good measure, pressed down, shaken together, and running over (see Lk. 6:38). We cannot truly love as long as we are only looking out for ourselves. Human nature will always strive to protect and preserve itself. The nature of the flesh is to make sure nobody takes advantage of us. If I forgive someone and he turns around and hurts me again in the same way, I'm probably not going to forgive him a second time, let alone a third. But if that's the way I act, I am not walking in God's love. As long as we are looking out only for ourselves, we will never know how to walk in love.

Selfishness is the greatest hindrance to loving others. Human flesh is supremely selfish; it always looks out for its own welfare first. There is no selfishness in the God-kind of love, however. This is why we cannot walk in the flesh and walk in love. We will never know how to love as long as we're more concerned about ourselves than we are about others. Love gives itself freely and places the welfare of others ahead of its own.

Tapping into the Source of Love

The reason God commands us to love is because love is His nature. Jesus said that He is the vine and we are the branches, and we must abide in Him (see Jn. 15:1-5). In other words, our life is in Him. He is love, and we must draw our love from Him. We don't have love to give by ourselves; our love comes from loving Him. Because He first loved us, we can love others. If you don't know how to love, draw near to Christ and receive His love. Once you receive Christ's love, you will be able to love others. Just as we can forgive others because Christ first forgave us, we can love others because He first loved us. We can love because He first loved us. We can forgive because He first forgave us. Our love comes from Him; otherwise, it isn't genuine love.

> ## People who don't know how to forgive don't know how to love.

Love and forgiveness are closely linked. A loving heart is a forgiving heart. Jesus said that if we do not forgive others, our heavenly Father will not forgive us (see Mt. 6:15). What a profound—and frightening—statement! If we don't forgive others, God won't forgive us. God commands us to forgive others because forgiveness brings healing. It's all one huge love test. People who don't know how to forgive don't know how to love.

If you struggle with forgiving others for what they've done in your life, you are struggling in your love walk without realizing it. Anytime you forgive people for what they've done, devils are bound, and love begins to grow. Anytime you forgive an injustice of the past, you open the door for God to make it up to you. Maybe you were molested or abused, and it's not fair, but God says if you will let it go, He will make it up to you. He even says that when the thief has been found out, he'll repay you seven-fold (see Prov. 6:31). It's a faith issue. Even when every fiber of my being resists forgiving, I will choose to forgive because I believe what God said about making it up to me when I do.

It's simple to do really. And although it is a matter of spiritual warfare, seemingly small acts often prove to be the most powerful weapons. Simply speaking kindly to someone who has offended you, or putting your arms around somebody who has hurt you can bring positive returns far out of proportion to the loving act itself. It's just another love test. Buying a gift for someone who has been talking badly about you at the office may be a small act—but it will yield gigantic rewards in the Kingdom of God. Bitterness toward those who have hurt you, on the other hand, will only open the door for the enemy to come into your life. Anytime there is a decrease in love, there is an increase in demonic activity. Whenever we judge someone else, we let the enemy come in. We open the door for him to wreak havoc in our lives and the lives of those we love.

People don't need to be judged; they need to be loved. The enemy has played us for fools and has had his way with the church for far too long. We need to focus on perfecting our love walk and leave the judging up to God. There's no telling what God will do in the next ninety days for the church, or for each of us as individuals, if we simply make up our minds to put Him first in every part of our lives and learn to grow up in His love. Be mindful. Determine to pass every love test to the glory and honor of God. Determine to grow up in Christ. Go for the advanced degree in the Lord's school of love. Move to the head of the love class and graduate with honors. It's important. Paul said that faith is good, and that hope is good, but that nothing compares to love.

LOVE MATTERS

CHAPTER FOUR

Transformed by Love

We will hold to the truth in love, becoming more and more in every way like Christ, who is the head of his body, the church. Under his direction, the whole body is fitted together perfectly. As each part does its own special work, it helps the other parts grow, so that the whole body is healthy and growing and full of love.

EPHESIANS 4:15-16 NLT

As we grow up in Christ we learn that love is selfless. Less self in our motives equals more love in our actions. Love does not consider its own rights, is not proud, and does not get offended. The more we grow, the more we learn that if we can walk in love, our entire life will change—and that if only a few more of us walked in love, the entire world would change. Love begins when we purpose to be the first to lay down our rights, our selfish motives, and our pride. Love requires each one of us to lay down our lives.

As we walk the path of love, we also learn that as soon as we take the first step, we are tested immediately! Sometimes the people who test us the most are those we love the most. They seem to know how best to get under our skin. And we want to be valued and respected most by those closest to us—certainly more so than by people we don't know so well or care so deeply about. The more we grow in love, the more we find that we must lay down our lives—and our pride—most completely in our own homes. When we are "at home" we tend to let down our guard and fall into old, childish patterns of selfishness. Our true level of maturity is revealed where our inner child is most likely to appear - around the hearth.

Perhaps we need to protect our hearths as much as we do our hearts! Proverbs 4:23 (NLT) tells us to "guard your heart, for it affects everything you do." I like how *The Message* puts it:

> Keep vigilant watch over your heart;
> that's where life starts.
> Don't talk out of both sides of your mouth;
> avoid careless banter, white lies, and gossip.
>
> PROVERBS 4:23-24 THE MESSAGE

How do we guard our hearts? By avoiding careless banter, white lies, and gossip. These are heart issues. And where we need to watch ourselves the most is when we are relaxing in the comfort and familiarity of our homes—around our own hearths. Imagine if everything you said in the privacy of your home determined the course of your life! Practice being disciplined with your thoughts and words on the home front, and it will be much easier to think and speak lovingly at church and on the job. Develop the habit of speaking kindly, and you will find that falling into the "pride of life" in other areas will become less of a problem.

Pride: The Enemy of Love

The reason some people have such a hard time forgiving others is because they have grown accustomed to slipping into the pride of life. They have learned to put on the pride of life instead of putting on love. Their minds say, "I can't believe they did that to me after all I have done for them." Forgiveness is a fruit of love, and like love, grows through cultivating holiness—wholesome, godly habits—in our hearts. We must constantly prune away the negative tendencies of our minds, taking every thought captive to the obedience of Christ (see 2 Cor. 10:5).

forgiveness is not a matter of desire; it is a matter of obedience.

Let me say it this way, forgiveness is not a matter of desire; it is a matter of obedience. I may desire to be obedient to God's will because I want to walk in the favor of God, but it is still a choice of my will and not a matter of how I feel. I don't forgive you because I want to; I forgive you so God will forgive me. I forgive you so I can walk in love, because I know love heals, love restores, and love brings life. If I can't forgive, I will never learn to love unconditionally; I will never learn to truly love and get along with myself. That's the crux of it right there. Sometimes loving others is simply a matter of loving and forgiving ourselves.

When we are caught up in pride, we work against ourselves. Pride is not only divisive interpersonally, but intra-personally as well. If pride rules my life, my heart becomes divided. Does my heart belong to God or to my self-will? Am I acting in God's interest or my own? A house divided will not stand. There is no room for love when pride is present. Pride pushes out all love. Pride will blind you to the truth. Pride will keep you from seeing, let alone admitting, that you are wrong. When was the last time you told someone you were sorry? When was the last time you asked for forgiveness?

Pride will isolate you. Pride will cause you to withdraw until you find yourself trapped in a prison of self-pity. Set yourself free from that prison by expressing love. How can you love yourself if you can't show some love to other people? Pride will cause you to run from the people you need the most. It's no wonder that God hates pride so much. Pride is the parent of strife, bitterness and unforgiveness. It's a medical fact that holding unforgiveness in your heart will weaken your immune system. Bitterness and resentment create a chemical poison in your nervous system that will allow disease to invade your body. When we choose to walk in love, we are actually serving our own best interests. Strife and division, on the other hand, steal our health as well as our happiness.

The Secret to Happiness: Getting Along

Walking in love gives God the opportunity to move in our lives. After all, how much fun is life if we can't get along with others? Former President Teddy Roosevelt believed that this was the secret to happiness. Make no mistake; if you're hard to get along with, you won't have a very happy life.

That's why Paul told us to pursue peace. In pursuing peace we find joy and contentment. Pursuing peace is also how we honor God. When we pursue strife and division, we are honoring the prince of chaos and deception, as well as dishonoring God. Strife is of the flesh, while love is of the Spirit of Jesus Christ. The reason you keep gossiping about somebody at work is because you're letting your flesh rule you. The reason you keep talking about the things that somebody did to you is because you still haven't let it go—you have not let love rule in your heart.

Pride causes us to talk about others behind their back. Jesus said, "Judge not, that you be not judged" (Mt. 7:1). Someone may even have asked you to forgive him or her, but you won't let it go because your pride won't let it go. It's pride that's keeping your marriage from being healed. It's unforgiveness that's stopping the flow of love in your life. It's stopping your miracle. It's stopping your breakthrough, and you'll never be happy until you just let it go. If you want God to use your life for His glory, you have to humble yourself. You have to lower yourself so He can raise you up. God can't bless anybody who is high and mighty. You have to get down so He can raise you up.

> ## *If you want God to use your life for His glory, you have to humble yourself.*

Before you gave your life to the Lord, you could not forgive people who hurt you, but now the Greater One lives inside you. Now you have the strength to forgive, and the strength to overlook every offense in your life. When you are leaning on the Lord, you can forgive. When you are leaning on the Lord, you can let it go. When you are leaning on the Lord, you can do all things through Christ who strengthens you (see Phil. 4:13).

The Power of Gratitude

While eating dinner in the home of a Pharisee named Simon, Jesus received the loving ministrations of a woman who had a reputation as a notorious sinner. Sensing Simon's objection, Jesus told the story about a man who loaned money to two different people. To one man he loaned five hundred pieces of silver, and to another, fifty pieces. Neither one could repay the debt, so he forgave them both. Then Jesus asked the question, "Who do you think loved this man the most?" Simon answered that it was the one who had been forgiven of the larger debt. Jesus then nailed home His point:

Do you see this woman? I came into your house. You did not give me any water for my feet, but she wet my feet with her tears and wiped them with her hair. You did not give me a kiss, but this woman, from the time I entered, has not stopped kissing my feet. You did not put oil on my head, but she has poured perfume on my feet. Therefore, I tell you, her many sins have been forgiven—for she loved much. But he who has been forgiven little loves little. Luke 7:44a-47 NIV

I can relate to this woman. When you have a past like mine, you're grateful for the blood of Jesus Christ that helps you get it behind you once and for all. Some churches are what I call "lily-white" churches. Everybody is just so clean; no one has ever been dirtied by sin or wants to be near those who have. But that's not how we should be. There are people who need our help because of what we've been through. That's the reason we are rejoicing in church, because we've been forgiven of so much in our lives. We love Him so much because He's forgiven us of such a large debt.

Taking time to appreciate all that we've been forgiven of also helps us to forgive others. Basking in God's great love toward us enables us to love other people. We can forgive others because He first forgave us. We can overlook other people's faults because He overlooks ours. You may say you love the Lord, but God wants to know if you love Him enough to overlook what others have done to you. You say you love the Lord, but unless you can love those whom you can see, how can you love a God you cannot see? Don't tell me you love God if you have an attitude with your neighbor, or a race of people, or your mother-in-law. Don't tell me you love God if you can't forgive someone in your family, or in your church, or where you work. You have to stop and ask yourself, "Do I need to make some changes?" Is this what Jesus would do?

If you make the decision to walk in love, you will have to overlook every offense that comes your way.

Whether you like it or not, people are going to hurt your feelings. They are going to lie to you, talk about you behind your back, and kick you when you're down. That's the way it is. Love, however, does not get offended. If you make the decision to walk in love, you will have to overlook every offense that comes your way. If you choose God's way, you will have to love people who talk about you and try to hurt you. But always remember, you will win in the end, because love never fails.

Never Underestimate Love

We have to love God with all our hearts and then make a decision to love the people around us. God has given us the formula for love: To love Him, to love ourselves, so that we can love our fellowman. That means we've got to put God first and make a decision to get under His umbrella of love so that we can love unlovable people. If I love God with of all my heart, the enemy can come against me, but He can't stop me. If I give in to my flesh, the enemy will trip me up every time. But if I'm walking in love, he cannot cause me to stumble and he will never defeat me. The gates of hell cannot stop me if I'm operating in God's love.

When you crucify your flesh every day, you learn to love people when it's not normal for you to love them. Even though it may not be natural for you to love folks of a different color or nationality or religion, the love of Christ will cause you to love them all. You might not love these people because they are not familiar to you, but let me tell you, the moment you put your arms around people who are different from you, something happens in your heart and in your life. Barriers are broken and you find that you have more in common with them than you have differences. You find that we are all of the same Spirit in Christ.

The Lord wants you to grow to the point where you're tolerant of those you don't understand and who don't understand you. If you will love people the way Jesus loves His Church, they'll want what you have. The problem with religion is that it has no love. If you ever fail in religion, you will be cast aside. In some religions, if you fail, you will be killed. Religion separates people. In fact, the very nature of religion creates bias, prejudice and discrimination. Religion says, "They are bad people because they are not one of us. In the name of God, let's do away with them." But my Bible says that God is no respecter of persons. He has no race, color, or ethnicity. He is Spirit, and we must worship Him in spirit and in truth.

Love is all that really matters. We need to steer clear of religious legalism. People get so confused about what is righteous. The Bible says that God is love. Jesus said that love fulfills all of the law. He said, "If you've seen Me, you've seen the Father" (Jn. 14:9). God is not trying to knock you in the head; He's trying to help you because He loves you. If He loved you when you were ignorant of His love, how much more will He love you when you receive His love and openly love Him in return? There will always be an absence of love in this world, and that is why the Lord came into it - to bring light, love, and healing. The truth of the matter is that love will heal you faster than anything else in your life.

Perhaps that is why God commands us to focus on love.

Love is our best hope for healing our hearts, our communities, and our nation. God wants us to learn to care more about others than we do ourselves. We must discipline our flesh to walk in love like we discipline our minds to learn. We must exercise our love like we do our muscles. While the flesh wants to get even, love lets others get ahead. Love lets traffic get in front of you. Love surrenders the parking space. Love picks up the trash of the neighbor who ran over your petunias.

Love is our best hope for healing our hearts, our communities, and our nation.

Don't ever underestimate the power of love. It will put a family back together when nothing else can. It will heal you when nothing else can. Jesus was love made flesh as much as He was the Word made flesh. He went from commanding all of heaven's armies to sleeping in a manger. Why would He do such a thing? Because that's what love does. Love gives. Love puts others first. Love will change your life. Love will change the world.

LOVE MATTERS

CHAPTER FIVE

Sowing Seeds of Love

> Give, and it shall be given unto you; good measure,
> pressed down, and shaken together, and running over.
>
> LUKE 6:38A KJV

It is a foundational truth in life that whatever you give out is what will come back to you. If you don't like the way your life is going today, you've got to stop and ask yourself, "What do I need to change? What am I sowing, because I don't like what I'm reaping?" We might not be able to change the way other people treat us, but we can change the way we treat other people. And we will soon discover that we'll never achieve lasting satisfaction until we learn to get along with other people and sow love into their lives.

The Golden Rule

There is a reason why some people succeed at everything they do, and why some people fail. No matter how good you are at what you do, if you can't get along with folks, you probably won't have great or lasting success. Basically, if people don't like you, they're not going to help you. If people don't trust you, they're not going to bless you. If you are not easy to get along with, you will have a hard time in business, marriage, relationships, finances, and all other areas of life as well. But if you get along well with others, your whole life will be better.

People who are hard to get along with almost always find difficulties coming their way. If you go to a store and are not treated well, chances are you won't be back. It's the same with relationships. If somebody on your job or in your neighborhood doesn't treat you well, you will stay away from that person. In any kind of relationship, whatever you give out is what you're going to get back. That's why Jesus said, "Do for others as you would like them to do for you" (Lk. 6:31 NLT). The way you treat others determines how others will treat you. If you don't like what you're reaping today, change what you're sowing.

What's the key to getting along with others? It's putting yourself in their place, instead of putting them in their place. It's about treating others the way you want to be treated—or better yet, how *they* want to be treated. Being a people person means you put yourself in someone else's place so you can relate to that person. If you do not relate well to other people, your success in life is going to be very limited.

Being a People Person

Being a people person means encouraging others because that's what you'd want them to do for you. If someone puts you down, you won't be able to relate to that person. When someone is critical and negative, you can't relate to him or her—worse, you won't even have the desire to try. Critical and negative people usually have very few friends, because they do not relate well to others. In fact, if you have critical and negative friends, chances are when the phone rings, you check the caller ID to see who's on the other end of the line.

Charismatic people don't think so much about themselves and how other people are going to meet their needs, or dwell on how their needs aren't being met. Instead, they focus on meeting the needs of others.

On the other hand, when people are encouraging to you, you want to be around them. When people lift you up, you want to spend time with them. Think about what it means to have a charismatic personality. Charismatic people are always reaching out and making an effort to put others at ease. Outgoing people make others feel good about themselves. They are magnets for attention because of how they make other people feel. These are the folks who are the "life of the party," making sure everyone is having a good time.

That's the key to being charismatic. Charismatic people don't think so much about themselves and how other people are going to meet their needs, or dwell on how their needs aren't being met. Instead, they focus on meeting the needs of others. The word *charismatic* can be interpreted simply as possessing "gifts of blessing and encouragement." If you are the kind of person who likes to encourage and lift up others, you will soon discover that others like to be around you. They want to be with you because they relate well to you. You make them feel good. And that's what being a people person is all about.

The Boomerang of Encouragement

The happiest people on earth are those who relate well to other people. No other people in the world are more joyful and fulfilled than those who encourage others. This is the law of sowing and reaping, of giving and receiving, right out of the Word of God. Whatever standard of measure we use with others is the standard by which our returns will be measured. You will never experience full success or happiness in this life until you learn to relate well with other people. Give and it shall be given to you.

But so often, here's what we do; we say things like, "I'm just too shy," or "It's not my nature." That may be so, but sometimes we have to change. No matter who we are, we all have a deep need to be loved. We all have a deep need to be appreciated. That's why it is so important to praise people. Let them know when they do a good job. Make them feel appreciated, whether it is your spouse, your children, someone you work with, or someone you don't even know who is doing a good job.

Treat others the way you want them to treat you. Encourage others the way you want to be encouraged. Love others the way you want to be loved. Do people have a difficult time getting along with you? If you don't know, just ask someone close to you, and he or she will tell you. Have you ever heard anyone say that you are difficult to deal with? Has anyone ever told you that you've got a bad attitude and that you need to go back to bed? If so, then you need to make some changes in your life.

Your success will be determined by the encouragement and appreciation you give out to other people on a daily basis.

If you want to become a people person, then you need to see people in a different light. You need to develop the kind of personality that lifts people up and encourages them. Your success is going to be determined by something you do on a daily basis. You can't become spiritually mature by only going to church once a week any more than you can experience healthy nutrition by only watching what you eat once a week. Ultimately, your success will be determined by the encouragement and appreciation you give out to other people on a daily basis.

People Are the Goal

When I first began in the ministry, I was a businessman. I knew how to take a problem and get the job done. My attitude was that people were obstacles to solving problems—they were keeping me from where God was trying to take me. Obviously, I had to change if I was going to be a pastor! If I was going to fulfill my destiny, I had to start treating people differently. I had to get down on my knees and pray, "God, You've got to give me grace, because these people are killing me! Lord, Jesus, You've got to help me see people through Your eyes."

As long as you are pushing to achieve your goals, you will run over people to accomplish what you want to accomplish. As long as you are focused on achievement for your own benefit, people will get hurt and you will end up achieving very little. But if you can make the shift to being more concerned about people than about progress, when you learn to be more concerned about others than about yourself, then the blessings of achievement will come back to you in an abundant harvest. Happiness will come into your life when you forget about trying to make yourself happy, and focus on bringing happiness to others. You can love people without leading them, but you cannot lead people without loving them.

We all know that people in leadership who are on a power trip are no fun to be around. You don't win people's hearts just by achieving your goals. You win people's hearts by helping them grow personally, and by being concerned about their lives. I learned that people don't care how much I know until they know how much I care. It doesn't matter what you've got going on, if people don't know you care about what's going on with them. When you show people how much you care for them, they'll be drawn to you. Your potential as a leader depends on the potential you are able to bring out in others. Stop trying to sell people on how wonderful you are, and begin selling people on how wonderful they are!

The Power of Praise

Those who are generous with praise and encouragement draw people and favor to themselves. They find themselves in positions of leadership. Natural leaders sow seeds of encouragement and reap loyalty and respect. They naturally command respect rather than demand it. Great leaders make others feel good about themselves. Their influence is great because they lead people by inspiration rather than by intimidation. If you want to be a good leader, you're going to have to learn the art of praise. It's almost as important to praise people as it is to praise

God. If it blesses God, think how much it blesses people! People have to be encouraged if they're going to excel. They've got to be praised if they're going to go to the next level.

Most of us were not raised with praise. If you were raised in a household where you received regular praise and encouragement growing up, you are in the minority. Far too many of us were raised in an environment of criticism, and then, sadly, we raise our own kids exactly the same way. We need to break that cycle. All people, and especially children, need to be encouraged if they are even going to begin to fulfill their potential. No matter who we are, we all need affirmation. We all need encouragement. And we all need praise. Too often too many of us are stingy with our praise. We need to build others up and encourage them.

To change our world we must change our words. If we really want to help others, we need to focus on looking for their strengths and encouraging them where they are strong. Unfortunately, more often than not, we tend to magnify a person's weaknesses, and then fall into the negative habit of talking about those weaknesses to others, or, if we are related to this person, criticizing him or her at every opportunity. It seems to be human nature that the closer we are to someone, the more we focus on weaknesses rather than strengths—the more we criticize rather than appreciate. But when we are critical of others, we stop all relationship possibilities.

One of the best ways you can help other people is to see the best in them and praise them for the best that you see. There is no better place to start this than at home. Focus on the good that you see and speak it out, whether with your spouse or your children. This is so powerful! Practice Philippians 4:8 (NLT), "Fix your thoughts on what is true and honorable and right. Think about things that are pure and lovely and admirable. Think about things that are excellent and worthy of praise." By focusing on those things that are praiseworthy, pretty soon that will be mostly what you see. Or maybe you feel that it's the people around you who are critical. Even here you have an opportunity to practice sowing and reaping. If *you* consistently focus on the positive, eventually they will begin to change their focus as well. Praise is contagious! The more you do it, the more of it you will hear everywhere you go!

> ## *Praise is contagious! The more you do it, the more of it you will hear everywhere you go!*

Even if you work for a boss or with coworkers who are critical, or, at best, stingy with words of encouragement, take a bold step and be the first to offer an encouraging word. It is amazing what a few kind words of praise will do to change the environment. That is why the Bible is so full of God's words of praise and encouragement for those who believe. It tills the soil to receive the seeds of love your heart longs to give as a Christian. After all, God's own love has been birthed in your heart and it longs to be shared. What drew you to God? Wasn't it the message of hope and reconciliation He offered because He saw your potential in Christ?

That is what love does. It focuses on bringing out the best in other people.

Meeting the Needs of Others

There are many ways to bring out the best in other people. Offering words of encouragement is certainly the most immediate thing you can do in any situation. But you can also look to meet their needs in many other ways as well. This can be challenging, because we are usually so focused on our own needs that we aren't used to thinking of giving rather than getting. We humans are selfish by nature. Meeting other people's needs before our own can feel like swimming up stream; it's just the opposite of what our natural man wants to do. Our natural man wants to focus on self, and that's about it. You can rock someone's world simply by asking what you can do to help, or seeing what needs to be done and doing it. These are the types of actions that speak louder than any words!

Every single day we must make a conscious effort to deposit good will into the lives of those around us. John Maxwell advises us always to give more than we expect to get back.

That's what God did through his Son, Jesus Christ. It's the law of sowing and reaping, giving and receiving. The Lord laid down his temporal life so that we might all have eternal life. Because He was able to lay down His life, He expects us to do the same thing as we learn to love selflessly.

God tells us through Paul that we are more than conquerors, made righteous and holy, and able to do all things. And because He speaks those things over us, He desires to hear us return those words to Him. "Lord, You are able to do all things. You have conquered every enemy! Your Name is above every name. You are Holy!" He showed us how to do unto others as we would have them do unto us. How much are you willing to do? Remember, people don't care how much you know until they know how much you care.

As Jean Anouilh said, "Love, above all else, is the gift of oneself."

Guarding Your Heart

Once you understand that your success is tied to the way you relate with others, how you invest in their lives, and seek to meet their needs, you'll begin to face some of the issues going on in your heart. Focusing on others will bring you face to face with yourself, simply because the way you relate to others is a good indication of what's going on in your own heart. You will be forced to look inside and ask yourself if there are changes you need to make or hurts that need healing. To continue to grow in Christ and find success in this life, you will have to learn to deal with your heart issues. Remember the counsel of Proverbs 4:23 (NKJV), "Keep your heart with all diligence, for out of it spring the issues of life." In other words, your success is tied to the condition of your heart.

You can break the negative cycles in your life if you deal with the issues in your heart. Challenge yourself to let go of any bitterness, to forgive, and to sow seeds of love, and watch your future change. Success will be determined by the thoughts you allow and the little decisions you make to walk in love. If you can change what is going on in your heart, then you can change your future, because if you can change the condition of your heart, you will change the way you treat other people.

Make a decision to treat people how you would like to be treated. This has proven to be profitable for the most successful businesses. Nordstrom's, for example, has a policy that the customer is always right. Their policy is to treat customers the way they want to be treated—to smile and be friendly no matter what. And the result speaks for itself. Customers are so loyal that Nordstrom's has become one of the most popular department stores in America. The truth is, that is the way we all want to be treated, whether on the job, at church, or in a relationship. It's a simple truth; whatever we sow, we will reap.

The key to healing your heart is to have a genuine relationship with the Lord. Let His love fill the holes and bind the wounds in your heart. Once His love has filled your heart, you can forgive others, and then you can begin to forgive yourself. Our capacity to accept and love others is determined by the degree to which we are able to love and accept ourselves. You will discover that as your relationship with the Lord grows, your ability to love yourself grows, as well as your ability to relate well with other people.

Addressing the heart issues that keep us from loving people is so important. We have already talked about the warning we received from John that if we don't love people, we don't truly love God. This truth alone makes clear the absolute importance of learning to love other people.

Staying Connected

It is being connected to others that brings life's greatest joys. Take time to build relationships. Take time to invest in people. The happiest people on earth are those who are focused on the people around them, and busy cultivating quality relationships. Look at some of the "disconnects" that might keep you from staying connected. Are you negative and critical? Are you selfish and demanding? Are you more focused on what people can do for you than on what you can do for other people? Be careful you're not pushing people away. Pay attention to how others respond to you.

Talent and abilities never guarantee success. Neither do a great education and hard work. These things might increase your odds, but if you don't know how to love people and contribute to their success, few people will be compelled to contribute to yours. They will put obstacles in your path rather than help you clear them away. But when you walk in love and know how to promote other people, great success and happiness will come to you sooner rather than later.

Learn to sow into the lives of others. It's never too late to turn your life around. Thank God for the good news that lets us know it's never too late to get things turned around in our lives. Start sowing some seeds of love today.

CHAPTER SIX

The Enemy of Love

Let all bitterness, wrath, anger, clamor, and evil speaking be put away from you, with all malice. And be kind to one another, tenderhearted, forgiving one another, just as God in Christ forgave you.

EPHESIANS 4:31-32

Pat Tillman was a professional football player for the Arizona Cardinals who, in response to the terrorist attacks of 9/11, turned down a $3.6 million contract in order to join the military. Unfortunately, he was killed while serving in Afghanistan. Because of the grievous circumstances, the cause of his death was not immediately disclosed. No, he wasn't captured, tortured, and executed by the enemy. It wasn't the opposition that shot and killed him; it was his own people. He got caught in friendly fire. An accident, but it still killed him. In the same way, we can love the Lord and serve faithfully as part of the Body of Christ, but also, if we're not careful, contribute to an equally dangerous "friendly fire" within the brethren.

I'm talking about the fire that can come out of our mouths; how we talk *about* people when they aren't present, and how we talk *to* them when they are. If we don't pay attention, we can be deceived into thinking we're doing God's work, and yet at the same time kill one another with the things we say. We have to be particularly diligent that we obey the Word, put God first, and stay kindhearted and tender toward one another, quickly forgiving, and not letting bitterness take root in our hearts.

We all know that it is the nature of the flesh to be harsh. When our flesh is in control, we become bitter if we don't get what we want, and condescending, or, at best, insensitive to others with our words. It is natural for us, in our sinful flesh, to get offended and to hold a grudge against people we might even claim to love. But the truth of the matter is that if we call Jesus the Lord of our life, He expects us to make changes. He expects us to modify our behavior. It begins by having a relationship with Him—by knowing Him intimately. It begins by saying, "Lord, not my will, but Your will be done."

God's love will always choose to embrace rather than to avoid.

Paul tells us about the power of love to override the nature of the flesh. God's love will always choose to embrace rather than to avoid. The love of God doesn't talk about people behind their backs, no matter what they've done. Love doesn't murmur and it doesn't backbite. Love should be at the root of all our motives. Paul said that we can have all the spiritual gifts in our life, but if we don't know how to love, we are nothing but a "clanging cymbal" (see 1 Cor. 13:1 NIV).

The Accuser of the Brethren

There is a reason why the enemy is called the accuser of the brethren (see Rev. 12:10). First of all, he accuses us before God of all of our sins and failures. Then he accuses us in our own spirit. We constantly battle thoughts of shame, guilt, and condemnation for any number of things. He shoots accusations at us that we aren't good enough, or can't do anything right, or that God couldn't possibly love somebody like us. No matter how long ago we gave our life to the Lord, we still hear these accusations every day in our mind. The enemy's main job is to accuse. He especially tries to get us to accuse God by saying things like, "Well, if God really loved me, why would He let me go through what I'm facing right now?" And he is often also successful in getting us to accuse our brothers and sisters in Christ.

One of Satan's primary strategies in these last days is to cause division between people and families. His plan is to divide churches, marriages, communities, and nations. Jesus said that if there is division, the enemy can conquer, because a house divided cannot stand (see Mt. 12:25). But He also said, "If two of you on earth agree about anything you ask for, it will be done for you by my Father in heaven" (Mt. 18:19 NIV). Where there is division, there is weakness. Where there is agreement, there is power and stability.

Walking in love is true spiritual warfare.

Walking in love is true spiritual warfare. It is major warfare to walk in love when people do not act lovingly toward you. That battle is fought in the spirit realm as well as in your flesh. Your natural self has no trouble loving people who love you, but just try to love people who talk about you behind your back. And try not to contribute to the backbiting in response. If you are not careful, you can be the instigator of deadly friendly fire. You might be a Christian and say you love God, yet also be involved in assassinating someone's reputation. That simply should not be.

The enemy knows that if we reach a place called the unity of the brethren, his arrows cannot touch us. He will become powerless. That is why he works overtime to divide Christians and families. His most successful strategy is to divide and conquer. There is no question that the enemy has put together his most powerful army for these last days. He knows he has but a short time left to wreak havoc on the earth. He's doing everything possible to keep the body of Christ separated and divided because he knows how powerful we can be when we work together to do good.

Don't Be a Pawn of the Enemy

The enemy constantly works through Christians to stop the work of God. If you are not cautious, you will stab a co-laborer with your own sword and think that you're doing the work of the Lord. If you are not alert, you will wound a fellow believer and think that you're a tool of the Holy Spirit. Even the great apostle Paul, while he was still known as Saul, persecuted Christians while thinking he was doing the work of God. The only way the enemy can defeat us is to divide us. Never let yourself play into his plan.

The enemy's main plan is for us to attack one another through faultfinding and gossip. But the truth of the matter is, as long as you walk in love, the enemy cannot prevail against you or the Church. The gates of hell will not prevail as long as we walk in love. Faith works by love (see Gal. 5:6). If we can master this love walk, we will have the faith we need as believers to do anything that God tells us to do. All we have to do is stop agreeing with the enemy when he tries to get us to find fault with each other. Let's make up our minds to be kind to one another, tenderhearted, and forgiving.

Why is that so challenging? Because these are not our natural feelings; they are choices we have to make. We have to tap into the love of God to walk in the power, love, and self-control we need to discipline our thoughts and words (see 2 Tim. 1:7). Choosing to be kind and tenderhearted can feel like getting down on the ground and doing push ups; it's *hard*! But if every time you hardened your heart you were told by the sergeant to "drop down and give me fifty," pretty soon you would train your heart to be tender. Forgiveness is not about a feeling you have; it's about a decision you make. It's about training your heart and mind to obey Christ.

The Lord is a wise Commander and Chief. He knows that any time we harden our hearts we make ourselves vulnerable to the enemy of our souls. His Word provides instruction on how to secure our forces against the enemy's devices and not give him a foothold in God's Kingdom—the Kingdom that resides in our hearts. Any time unforgiveness or offense creeps up to the borders of our heart—any time faultfinding or gossip begins digging a trench outside the walls of our inner city—we open the gate for the enemy to come into our lives to kill, steal, and destroy.

Many times, the root of division has to do with pride. Pride is a hallmark trait of the enemy. Satan put himself above God because of his pride. Do you see how deceptive pride can be? It will cause you to think that you are better than other people; that you are wiser than others, even God. Because you are self-deceived—"blinded by pride," so to speak—you will begin to think you deserve more, and are entitled and justified to do whatever satisfies your desires. You will become ever more self-seeking and self-promoting. You will find yourself walking more in the flesh than in love, becoming easily offended and critical. Now you too become an accuser of the brethren; and, just like Satan, you will be cast down.

Pride Comes before a Fall

It is after our greatest victories that we are most vulnerable to pride. Pride rises up to snatch control after God helps you land that big contract, or build that big church, or buy that new house. It sneaks up on you after you finally get to sing a solo, or are promoted, or recognized for some minor accomplishment. All of a sudden you are something special. The whole world seems to acknowledge your giftedness, and you become a little more confident in your own abilities. Of course, confidence is not a bad thing, as long as it is rooted in Christ. Otherwise, everything you do to lift yourself up will eventually result in your downfall. Why? Because God opposes the proud. Only by giving God the glory for all you achieve, and by humbling yourself before Him, will you be raised up.

It is what we do to glorify the Lord Jesus Christ that results in our going to the next level, in whatever area of our lives - our ministries, our professions, or our passions. Every failure we experience is a result of trusting in ourselves more than the

Lord. But sometimes failure can be the catalyst that turns us around; a wake up call to humble us before God. Failure can be our path to greater faith when we realize that God will take what the enemy meant to hurt us, and use it for our good.

> *Failure can be our path to greater faith when we realize that God will take what the enemy meant to hurt us, and use it for our good.*

How do you define success? Do you consider success to be building a big church or a great ministry? Or do you consider it to be having an ever-deepening relationship with the Lord? This is what Paul had to say at the end of his life, "That I may know Him and the power of His resurrection, and the fellowship of His sufferings, being conformed to His death" (Phil. 3:10). In the end, success is not about any great achievement other than knowing Christ, the power of His resurrection, and the fellowship of His suffering. The Lord doesn't want you singing for Him unless you know Him, because it's not about singing a solo. Singing a solo can be about selfish ambition. We need to be set free from selfish ambition and competition. Paul said, "I have been crucified with Christ; it is no longer I who live, but Christ lives in me" (Gal. 2:20a).

The voice that is telling you that you need to be recognized and promoted is not the voice of God. If you are bent out of shape because nobody is patting you on the back, be careful, because pride is lying at your door trying to set a trap for you. Pride always goes before the fall (see Prov. 16:18). The higher you go in the Lord, the farther you can fall if you don't crucify your flesh every single day. That's why you have to make up your mind to deny yourself, love the Lord with all your heart, *and* love your neighbor as yourself. What does that mean? It means you need to put God first, and forgive people you don't want to forgive. Do that, and God will lift you up.

Overcoming Evil

Even if your hopes are dashed and you run out of faith, love will get you through. Love is the greatest weapon we have to overcome the problems in our lives. Remember, God's Word tells us that love never fails (see 1 Cor. 13:8), and that we overcome evil with good (see Rom. 12:21), because love is stronger than hate. Don't let bitterness take root in your heart or it will entangle you. If you learn to forgive people instantly, the love of God will see you through to victory every time. As I've said before, God has promised that if you will forgive those who have hurt you, he will make it up to you. As long as you walk in God's love, you will never fall prey to the enemy or be used as his pawn to hurt other people.

That is why Jesus placed such importance on this one issue. In Romans 13:8, Paul says that love fulfills all the commandments. Jesus told us specifically to "love one another as I have loved you" (Jn. 15:12). In John 13:34-35 He spells it out more plainly still, "A new commandment I give to you, that you love one another; as I have loved you, that you also love one another. By this all will know that you are My disciples, if you have love for one another."

It's easy to love someone who loves you, but how do you respond when someone does something that hurts you or offends you? If you are crucified with Christ, then you don't get offended. If you're crucified with Christ, you embrace somebody you would not normally embrace. I'm talking about overcoming every work of darkness simply by walking in the love of God. If you've got a chip on your shoulder, then you're not walking in God's love. If you're finding fault with others, you're not walking in God's love. The truth of the matter is, when you are critical, what you're really doing is setting yourself up as judge and executioner. As we have already seen, the Bible is clear about what will happen when you judge and condemn other people; you will suffer the same temptation and bring the same judgment back upon yourself (see Mt. 7:1-2.)

But the Lord is merciful and does not want us to suffer that condemnation. God wants to protect us by teaching us how to love. Jesus commanded that we love God with all of our heart, soul, mind, and strength (see Mk. 12:30; Lk. 10:27), that we might be empowered to love our fellow man as ourselves. We can resist gossiping because God's love covers a multitude of sins. We can refuse to criticize a fellow believer so as not to become a tool of the enemy. The enemy knows that love never fails. He knows that if we overlook all offenses, we're going to have a tremendous amount of spiritual strength in our lives. Even the enemy knows that the greatest power on earth is the power of God's love.

Love^2 = 7Power

I learned something a few years ago that absolutely revolutionized my life. I'd been praying things like, "God, demonstrate Your power so the people believe in You. God, demonstrate Your miracles so the people will know who You are." But God showed something to me. God revealed to me that He never demonstrates His power so people will believe in Him—He demonstrates His power so people will know of His great love for them. God's aim is to convince people of His love for them, so that they will open their hearts to love Him with their entire being. If we can yield to His love—find our confidence in His love—then we can become instruments of His love. Then we will reach out our hands to the sick and they will recover. We will pour out our souls to comfort the afflicted, and only then will we lay down our lives to set the captives free.

Our goal should be to walk in the power of God's love, not walk in the love of God's power. The truth is, if you walk in

God's love, you will ultimately experience God's power. Moreover, without a revelation of that love, you will forever remain powerless. That is why we must seek His love more than we seek His power. We really only need to be asking the Lord one thing - how to better love Him and His people. We must daily cry out to God that He teach us how to love.

If you are fasting and praying for a miracle, you should be fasting and praying for more love so that the miracles can come. What good is it to have the power for miracles if you don't have the power to love? The world won't know us by our spiritual gifts, or by our doctrines, or by the size of our buildings; the world will know us by our love for the Lord and for each other. The world will know us because we are selfless, kindhearted, and forgiving. We will never succeed in cultivating the fruit of the Spirit in our lives (see Gal. 5:22-23) without cultivating love, which is the first spiritual fruit and the key to all the others.

Remember Paul's words, "If I have all faith, so as to remove mountains, but do not have love, I am nothing. And if I give all my possessions to feed the poor, and if I surrender my body to be burned, but do not have love, it profits me nothing" (1 Cor. 13:2-3 NASB). We don't need more power; we need more love.

Turning It All Around

If you will walk close to the Lord everyday, He will take what the enemy meant to hurt you and turn it for your good.

Every wound that you receive will eventually result in someone else's blessing. It is certain that you will get wounded in this life. People will talk about you and then lie to your face about being your friend. The truth of the matter is that every wound you receive can be used to bring healing to somebody else. It is by the Lord's stripes that we are healed, but it is through our stripes that we are given authority to heal others.

> ### *It is by the Lord's stripes that we are healed, but it is through our stripes that we are given authority to heal others.*

Wherever you have been wounded is the very area that God empowers you to heal others. Whatever you have gone through, God wants to bring healing to you so that you can bring healing to others. God uses our wounds to lead us to our ministries. If you want to know what your ministry is, look at your woundings; look at the things you've gone through and know that that is where God wants to use you. Somebody's healing depends on you.

If we are going to be victorious in these last days, we have to learn to overcome evil with the power of God's love. If we are wise to the ways of God, we will cover every sin with a blanket of love and use every hurt as a bridge to reach the suffering.

The greatest weapon we have against the kingdom of darkness is the power of God's love. When we're facing a difficult situation, we need to stop and ask, "What would Jesus do?" The root of all our shortcomings is that we don't know how to walk in the love of God. We say we love each other, but we talk about one another's faults, passing blame, and lifting ourselves up at the expense of our brothers and sisters in Christ.

Paul said, "Now abide faith, hope, and love, these three; but the greatest of these is love" (1 Cor. 13:13). Hope is good. We have hope in the Lord. Faith is good. We have to have faith in the Lord. But love is the greatest of all.

CHAPTER SEVEN

The Love Cure

> Most important of all, continue to show deep love for
> each other, for love covers a multitude of sins.
>
> 1 Peter 4:8 NLT

Not only does love cover a multitude of sins; it heals a multitude of hurts. And all of us, no matter who we are, are nothing more than hurting sinners. No matter how beautiful we are, we struggle with heartaches. No matter how rich we are, we all have burdens in our lives. We all suffer from a myriad of temptations and bad habits. Some people might look like they have it all together on the outside, but that doesn't mean they're not struggling with debilitating issues on the inside.

Unfortunately, more often than not, pride keeps us from admitting that we're going through something difficult and need help. James told us to confess our sins to one another so we could pray for each other and be healed (see Jas. 5:16.) Instead, we pretend that everything is fine. We wear a holy mask

85

and think we're deceiving those around us, when we're really only deceiving ourselves.

Do not be deceived! No matter what burden you are facing, no matter what difficulty you are dealing with, you cannot overcome it if you will not confront it. As long as you sweep it under the rug, you will not be able to defeat it. You need to begin by taking off that mask and getting real before God and the saints around you. God wants to bring healing to you, and often that healing comes through His Body here in the earth. For each of us, that body is the local church.

Coming Clean

One of the greatest things about our God is that no matter who we are or what we have done, He will never leave us or quit on us. God will continue doing everything He can to help us overcome and put behind us whatever has held us back. We are only required to do one thing; Come clean before God and our brethren. Sometimes we must begin by facing ourselves—taking a good look in the mirror and speaking truth to ourselves. One of the most difficult things can be confronting ourselves about the issues the Lord has put on our hearts. God is trying to get our attention. It's time for change. It's time for us to confront our problems and make things different.

The Word of God says that if we will judge ourselves, God won't have to (see 1 Cor. 11:31). What is your burden today?

What are the issues that you need help with? Many are the afflictions, or troubles, or burdens of the righteous, but the Lord shall deliver you out of them all. (see Ps. 34:19.) If you're in a desperate situation, be assured that God does His best work in your darkest hour. God does His best work when your back is up against the wall. That's the kind of God we serve.

But you also have a spiritual enemy who is trying to convince you that nothing is ever going to change in your life. You have an enemy who is trying to keep you from getting involved in your church. He is doing everything he can to stop you from growing in your faith. The enemy's plan is to isolate you and make you think that you will never be happy again. He wants you to feel sorry for yourself and believe that nobody loves you, and to become so hopeless that he can steal your future.

> *The source of our healing is God's Word and Jesus Christ, but faith for that healing will be stirred through involvement in a local church.*

But I am here to serve an eviction notice on the enemy of your soul! The Lord gave me a word some time ago, and He spoke to my heart and said that your healing is going to come through the Body of Christ. Now don't misunderstand me;

the source of our healing is God's Word and Jesus Christ, but faith for that healing will be stirred through involvement in a local church. If you'll get hooked into your local church, your healing or provision or whatever you need will come to pass in your life.

We Are of One Body

The Word says that when one member of the Body suffers, we all suffer. How can the foot say to the hand, "I don't need you"? If we are born again, we are all part of the Body of Christ, and we are supposed to lay hands on one another, put our arms around each other, and lift one another up. Once we understand that we are all part of one body, we will stop criticizing and murmuring about others in the church.

The bottom line is this, when you hurt someone else as a believer in the body, you're also hurting yourself. For one thing, whatever you sow you will reap. Whatever criticism you have of other people will come back on you. Whenever you are judgmental or insensitive, people will be judgmental and insensitive towards you. It's a no-win situation. If you want to go higher in the Lord, you've got to quit finding fault with others.

One Sunday when I preached on this, my wife was home sick. I got on the phone with her, and the next thing you know, there we were finding fault with somebody! The pastor had hardly left the church, and here I was having this conversation with my wife. I said to her, "Baby, if you had been in church this morning, we wouldn't be having this conversation!" We all need help! The spirit is willing but the flesh is weak. We find fault all the time and don't even realize it. We think we're just telling the truth, but that is only an excuse. If you ask God, He will set off a little alarm inside of you when you start finding fault with other people, so you can stop before you even begin!

If you are looking for God to do a miracle in your life, you will have to pass the love test. Faith works by love. If your love isn't working, your faith isn't going to work. James told us to pray for one another so that we can be healed. We are to give to each other what we need ourselves. We have to give to each other if we're going to expect God to give back to us. We're supposed to restore one another in a spirit of gentleness, bear one another's burdens, and believe the best of each other, while also preferring one another in love. God says that we're not supposed to judge each other, but to love one another.

So why are we accusing one another? Why do we point our fingers at others? Listen to what the Lord said through Isaiah:

> Then you will call, and the Lord will answer; you
> will cry for help, and he will say: Here am I. "If
> you do away with the yoke of oppression, with
> the pointing finger and malicious talk…then your

light will rise in the darkness, and your night will
become like noonday."

Isaiah 58:9-10 NIV

The Lord will answer us if we stop talking negatively about
one another. His deepest desire is that we would walk in love
and unity and peace with one another. Paul said it this way,

"Aim for restoration, comfort one another, agree with one
another, live in peace; and the God of love and peace will be
with you" (2 Corinthians 13:11 ESV). If we can understand
that every single one of us is hurting in some way—that we are
all broken in an area, or two, or three, in our lives—and that
we all need God's healing in our lives, perhaps then we will be
able to conduct ourselves with compassion, even in the privacy
of our own thoughts.

Edifying Ourselves in the Love of God

Love will heal you when nothing else can. You can be tired,
discouraged, maybe even a little depressed, and someone of-
fers a hug. Then maybe you see another friend and offer him or
her a hug, and before long, you feel encouraged and energized.
We have heard it said, "No man is an island." That means we
are not meant to deal with our problems alone. The reason the
Lord wants us to bear each others burdens is because of the
strength that comes to us when we stand with each other. One
can put a thousand to flight, but two can put ten thousand to
flight (see Deut. 32:30). In other words, by myself I've got a

certain amount of power in the spiritual realm, but when you stand with me it's multiplied tenfold!

The Bible tells us that there is great power in agreement. Jesus said, "If two of you agree down here on earth concerning anything you ask, my Father in heaven will do it for you" (Mt. 18:19 NLT). For that reason alone, it is important to keep the peace in your home! Your prayers will not be answered as long as there is strife and unforgiveness. It is so important to stay in agreement with your marriage partner and your business partner. A house—or a company—divided cannot stand. You've got to make up your mind to do everything you can to bring peace into your personal and professional relationships, settle your issues, give up quarreling, and walk in agreement with people.

You say you love the Lord, but you have all sorts of problems with people. Maybe your problem is with your flesh and not with other people. Take a good look at yourself and see if maybe you don't have some issues you need to work out within yourself. No matter what you find that is causing you to stumble, take it before the Lord and confess it to Him. You can keep it just between you and Him, but stop sweeping it under the rug. First John 1:9 (NIV) assures us, "If we confess our sins, he is faithful and just and will forgive us our sins and purify us from all unrighteousness." Whatever your issue, whatever your burden, whatever you are carrying, if you will confess it to Him, He will lift it from you and you will be set free from it.

The problem is that we try to carry these things alone—
we try to pick ourselves up by our own bootstraps, so to speak.
But God didn't create us that way. We can't make it by ourselves. We need the Lord, and we need the Body of Christ to
see us through.

After you have come clean with the Lord, wait on Him for
new strength. Trust Him to give you what you need to overcome. Cast your care upon Him and let Him bear the burden
for you (see 1 Pet. 5:7.) "Do not be anxious about anything,
but in everything, by prayer and petition, with thanksgiving,
present your requests to God. And the peace of God, which
transcends all understanding, will guard your hearts and your
minds in Christ Jesus" (Phil. 4:6-7 NIV).

God wants you to learn to trust in Him in the middle of
your storm. But God also knows that until you come to the end
of yourself, you will never really be able to trust Him with your
whole heart. Until you are finally able to say, "Lord, I give up! I give
it *all* over to You!" He can't do much for you. It is when you come
to the end of yourself that God can move into your life. I don't
know about you, but I'm not too proud to say, "Lord, I'm weak
and I need Your help!" I'm not too proud to say, "Lord, my burdens are so heavy, I can't make it if you don't take them from me."

Those burdens are part of God's plan. No, His purpose
is not to create burdens for you, but He will use them to

bring you to the end of yourself. They are part of God's plan to bring you closer to Him. Sometimes the hardest thing is learning to trust in His wisdom and strength rather than our own. The tendency of our flesh is to be our own god, but when the burdens and pressures come bearing down, threatening to crush us, that's when we are forced to face up to our weaknesses. That's when we finally turn it all over to God. We need to be humbled by the world sometimes, just so the Lord can lift us up. When we experience God's redemptive power, there is nothing on this earth that can disconnect us from His love.

> *When we experience God's redemptive power, there is nothing on this earth that can disconnect us from His love.*

Bearing One Another's Burdens

C. S. Lewis said that the greatest sin in the church today is that of judging others. God hasn't called us to judge one another; He's called us to love one another. Jesus provided the example; He walked ahead of us, showing us how to live among one another. He is the "Great Burden-bearer." He said, "Come to Me, all you who labor and are heavy laden, and I will give you rest" (Mt. 11:28).

He has called us to hold one another's hands and to bear each other's burdens. While religion condemns people, Christ lifts people out of their burdens. There is no condemnation for those who are in Christ Jesus—there is no condemning sentence for anyone who loves the Lord. When you understand that there is "none righteous, no not one" (Rom. 3:10), then you will understand that every one of us is guilty of something. When you understand that you have no right to judge anyone, then you will grab your neighbors by the hand and pray for them, and help bear their burdens.

The story of the Good Samaritan tells of religious people who saw a man who was hurting, but did not want to help him because he was not one of their kind. There is no love in religion, but Jesus came to bring us love. The Good Samaritan, like Christ, picked up the hurting man, bandaged his wounds, and lifted his burdens. When we send our rapid response team out on the streets in zero-degree weather to minister to the homeless, what we're saying is, "God loves you and we're here to help bear your burdens." Delivering food to the poor says, "We love you and we're here to bear your burdens with you." When folks go into the prisons, they're saying, "We love you. We're here to help bear your burdens and let you know that God isn't mad at you."

The woman caught in the act of adultery was brought before Jesus. The religious people wanted to kill her, but Jesus wanted to save her. He reached down in the dirt, picked her up, put His arms around her, and began to show her love. Isn't that what God has called us to do, to pick up people that are hurting and to wrap our arms around them? That's what love does. Love does not judge. Love says, "Let me pick you up. Let me put my arms around you. Let me pray for you."

Christianity is supposed to be kind, not judgmental. Christianity is supposed to be about loving one another and bearing each other's burdens. Paul prayed that there would be no divisions among us because he knew that the enemy's plan was to separate and to divide people. Satan will use anything he can to keep us apart. He'll spread lies. He'll even spread the truth, if it will help his cause. He doesn't care, as long as people stay disconnected and powerless.

The Christian army is notorious for kicking its soldiers when they're down—for casting out its wounded instead of restoring them. But instead of helping the enemy destroy one another, shouldn't we be holding each other's arms up? Shouldn't we be bearing one another's burdens? Shouldn't we be praying for one another rather than passing judgment on each other?

It's time for Christ's Body—His Church—to get into the flow of God's love. We were not created to hate; we were created to love. We were not created to tell people off or give them a piece of our mind. We were created to be instruments of love, because love brings healing to people. Remember Jesus' words, "A new commandment I give to you, that you love one another; as I have loved you, that you also love one another. By this all will know that you are My disciples, if you have love for one another" (Jn. 13:34-35). If you're a disciple of Jesus Christ, you won't condemn the hurting and burdened; you will love them.

Love, Liberty, and Life

> Whenever you stand praying, if you have anything
> against anyone, forgive him, that your Father in heav-
> en may also forgive you your trespasses. But if you do
> not forgive, neither will your Father in heaven forgive
> your trespasses.
>
> MARK 11:25-26

If you never understand anything else in the kingdom of
God, you have to understand this one thing; condemnation
(unforgiveness) is the nature of Satan, while mercy (forgiveness) is the nature of God. There is nothing but darkness
where there is unforgiveness, and nothing but hope and light
where there is mercy. If you are a believer, and have given your
life to the Lord Jesus Christ, God expects you to be different from how you were before you moved to the Kingdom of
Light. The law of the land is that you walk in love, and that
requires you to forgive. God tells us that if we are willing and
obedient, we will eat the good of the land (see Is. 1:19.) God

says He wants us to be blessed and have the best, but in order to receive that, we have to be willing to obey His Word.

Teaching obedience is one of our biggest challenges as parents. We love our children so much and have only their very best at heart. But we know that if they are disobedient they will never experience our best intentions for them. They have to learn self-discipline, responsibility, courtesy, and respect if they are going to succeed in life. If we as earthly parents want the best for our kids, and go to great lengths to teach good values and develop character in our children, how much more does our Heavenly Father want the best for us? How much farther will He go to develop His righteousness and character in us? How much liberty and life do you think God the Father wants for those who love Him?

Growing Up and Living Free

Many of us, before we gave our lives to the Lord, were selfish and hateful. We copped an attitude when people did us wrong, and held onto that attitude for a long time. After we came to know the love of God, we were able to show mercy through His Spirit. Our Heavenly Father expects us, with the help of the Holy Spirit, to rise above our flesh and grow up in Christ. He commands us to bless those that persecute us—to bless them and not curse them! (see Rom. 12:14.) He instructs us to "Let all bitterness, wrath, anger, clamor, and evil speaking be put away from you, with all malice. And be kind to one another, tenderhearted, forgiving one another, just as God in Christ forgave you" (Eph. 4:31-32). He urges us to get along by "bearing with one another, and forgiving one another, if anyone has a complaint against another; even as Christ forgave you, so you also must do" (Col. 3:13). If we will learn to obey Him, He will bless us.

But even as Christians we tend to say, "Well I will forgive, but I'm not going to forget!" We want to hold people hostage for the things they've done to us. The problem is, anytime you hold something against somebody else, you are actually the one being held hostage. You will never truly be free as long as you hold on to those grudges.

Unforgiveness is a sticky thing; it ties you to the people who have hurt you.

Unforgiveness is a sticky thing; it ties you to the people who have hurt you. It's like a binding cord you need to cut loose before it turns into a noose around your neck! You are tied emotionally to the person you have not forgiven, and are dragging that person around with you like a corpse. He or she is completely unconscious of your burden; totally unaware of being dragged around with you wherever you go. That kind of burden will wear you out, and never touch the person you're holding a grudge against. You won't understand why you're so exhausted all of the time, but it's because you're dragging around a dead weight that you don't need to be carrying. By tying yourself to the very person you despise and want out of your life, you have imprisoned yourself with that person—except that you are the only one who is bound.

In other words, by refusing to forgive, you make yourself a slave to the person who hurt you. Why would you want to give that person so much power over you? If you want that person out of your life, you have to forgive him or her once and for all. Release the one who hurt you, and then God can release you.

Have you ever met people who have a hard time forgiving themselves? That is because they are reaping what they have sown. They have not been able to forgive others and so now they can't even forgive themselves. You may hate someone and never want to see that person again, but your lack of forgiveness will tie you emotionally to your offender for years. Somebody may have abused you in the past, but because you won't let it go, you're tormented with the thought of that person for the rest of your life. The answer is forgiveness. That is why you have to forgive the abusers and the molesters—people who don't deserve to be forgiven. It's not about them. It's all about you being free from the bondage of unforgiveness.

A Hard Lesson

Jesus told a story in the eighteenth chapter of Matthew about a king who compassionately forgave the debt of one of his servants—a debt so large it would have been impossible to repay. The forgiven servant immediately went out in pursuit of a debt owed him by another of the king's servants. This debt was quite small, yet the forgiven servant was deaf to the pleas of his fellow servant for more time to pay. Instead, the forgiven servant had the other man thrown into debtors' prison. All this over a debt that amounted to a few dollars! This classic parable is worth repeating because the message seems so easily forgotten. Listen carefully to what happened next, and pay heed to the lesson we need to learn again and again:

Then his master, after he had called him, said to him, "You wicked servant! I forgave you all that debt because you begged me. Should you not also have had compassion on your fellow servant, just as I had pity on you?" And his master was angry, and delivered him to the torturers until he should pay all that was due to him. So My heavenly Father also will do to you if each of you, from his heart, does not forgive his brother his trespasses.
Matthew 18:32-35

Jesus said, "My heavenly Father will not forgive you if you don't forgive your fellow man." Anytime you get your feelings hurt, you've got to decide whether you're going to hang on to it or whether you're going to let it go. Is it so important that you would give up God's mercy toward you? Is it worth losing out on the forgiveness of your Heavenly Father just to keep that chip on your shoulder? Certainly we can't help getting wounded, but we don't have to stay wounded. We can give it to God and choose to forgive.

It's a faith issue. Truly forgiving people who don't deserve to be forgiven exercises our faith. We know that the just shall walk by faith and not by sight (see 2 Cor. 5:7), and that it is impossible to please God without faith (see Heb. 11:6). When we forgive somebody who doesn't deserve to be forgiven, we are choosing to fight the good fight, and we are choosing to please God. Keep in mind, however, that even though the person who hurt you may not deserve forgiveness, neither do you. None of us deserve forgiveness, yet God forgave us. And he expects no less of us as His children.

On the flip side, if we choose not to forgive, Jesus said we would be turned over to the tormentors! What are the tormentors? Bitterness, strife, hate—all of these are of the enemy. James said that where there is strife and division there is confusion and every evil thing! (see Jas. 3:16.) Unforgiveness will cause strife and division; it will cause you to be anxious and troubled. It will cause you to lose sleep. It will cause your health to deteriorate and erode your emotional and mental well-being. You allow the tormentors to eat you alive simply because someone offended you or hurt you in some way. No hurt inflicted on you by someone else can begin to compare to the havoc unforgiveness will wreak in your life. But the moment you let go of those people who have hurt you, the moment you release them from your heart, they can't hurt you anymore.

> *Whatever you loose people from on earth,*
> *you are loosed from in heaven,*
> *but whatever you hold against others,*
> *God holds against you.*

Letting Loose

Jesus said, "Whatever you bind on earth will be bound in heaven, and whatever you loose on earth will be loosed in heaven" (Mt. 18:18). Another way to say this is, "Whatever you hold against people on earth, God holds against you in heaven." You'll never really make any progress as long as you hold something against someone on earth. Your success will be bound up in heaven until you break free from the bondage of unforgiveness in your life.

This principle of binding and loosing is one of the keys to the Kingdom of Heaven that Jesus talks about in Matthew chapter eighteen. In this chapter, Jesus maps it all out for us and shows us plainly how the Kingdom operates. If you need a breakthrough in your life, you must understand this one principle, whatever you bind on earth is bound in heaven, and whatever you loose on earth is loosed in heaven. In other words, whatever you loose people from on earth, you are loosed from in heaven, but whatever you hold against others, God holds against you. You need to break free.

If you are not experiencing victory in your life, you need to stop and ask yourself, "Is it because I keep holding onto bitterness? Is it because I keep talking about folks behind their back and it's coming back to me?" If you have been praying for God to heal you and nothing has happened, it could be because whatever you bind on earth is bound in heaven. The heavens are all bound up because you won't believe other people, because you badmouth them, and because you refuse to forgive them.

Remember that life and death are in the power of the tongue (see Prov. 18:21.) We must be very careful about talking about folks behind their backs. If you are constantly facing health challenges, check your heart and the words that are coming from your mouth. You might be catching more colds than anybody else because of your attitude. Unforgiveness weakens your immune system. Perhaps the doctor can't find anything wrong with you, even after running all kinds of tests. It could be that the unforgiveness in your heart is making you sick. Instead of criticizing others, you need to "guard your heart, for it affects everything you do" (Prov. 4:23 NLT). You can get things turned around if you will listen to God and hear what He is telling you.

Faith and Obedience

When you forgive people who don't deserve it, you are demonstrating that you are a person of faith. Forgiving undeserving people shows that you love the Lord. Forgiveness is a command, not an option. At heart, forgiveness is an issue of faith and obedience. It takes faith to forgive. It takes faith to release others and believe that God will turn it for your good. The Bible says that faith works by love. Your faith won't work if your love isn't working, and where there is unforgiveness, there is no love.

Jesus told us to forgive others so our heavenly Father would forgive us (see Mk. 11:25-26). In the Model Prayer, or "Lord's Prayer", He taught us to pray, "And forgive us our debts, as we forgive our debtors" (Mt. 6:12). We all must go to God for forgiveness. Whether we're the pastor or the plumber, we all need forgiveness, but we all also must forgive others if we expect to be forgiven ourselves.

Jesus hung on a cross. His executioners drove spikes through His hands and His feet. But before that, they beat Him. They ripped the skin off of His back and shoved a crown of thorns on His head. They pulled out His beard. They spat on Him. They humiliated Him by stripping Him naked, and made fun of Him. Yet as He hung there on the cross, Jesus said, "Father, forgive them, for they do not know what they do" (Lk. 23:34).

If Jesus, being obedient unto death, could forgive his persecutors who hated and tormented Him, shouldn't we be able to forgive our brothers and sisters in Christ?

If Jesus, being obedient unto death, could forgive his persecutors who hated and tormented Him, shouldn't we be able to forgive our brothers and sisters in Christ?

With some of His final words, Jesus forgave His tormentors. He died on a Friday, and it seemed like it was all over. By the time Sunday morning came, however, Jesus' enemies had been silenced. You may be hanging on a cross of your own today, but if you'll forgive, Sunday will come in your life. If you'll make up your mind to release others from the things they've done to you, so many distractions in your life will be silenced. If you'll let go of the past, there's no telling what God will do for you in the future.

The people Jesus forgave on the cross did not deserve forgiveness. Yet that is the very criterion we so often try to apply. When somebody hurts us, we are quick to say, "He or she doesn't deserve to be forgiven." But that is not the issue. As I said before, none of us deserve forgiveness, no matter who we are. So whether or not a person deserves forgiveness is beside the point. The point is whether or not we will obey God, walk in faith, and forgive. The issue is whether we will forgive so that God can forgive us and answer our prayers. This is absolutely essential to becoming spiritually mature.

The Simplicity of Holiness

I know of a particular group of people that call themselves the "holiness denomination." These folks wear plain clothes, the women wear their hair in buns, they refuse to listen to music, and rarely smile. But holiness is not about being somber and wearing your hair in a bun. Holiness is about putting God first in all things. Holiness is about forgiving folks who don't deserve to be forgiven.

God wants us to forgive others no matter what they've done to us. He wants us to release all the pain and cancel every debt so that we can walk in freedom. I don't know about you, but I need heaven's power working in my life too desperately to tie it up with unforgiveness.

Peter put it this way, "As He who called you is holy, you also be holy in all your conduct, because it is written, 'Be holy, for I am holy'" (1 Pet. 1:15-16). "All your conduct" refers to our behavior and manner of living, but it is determined by the thoughts in our hearts and the words in our mouths. If we can keep the sin of unforgiveness out of our heart, than we can keep the critical words from falling out of our mouths.

Holiness is simple. It's about keeping your heart clean before God.

Holiness is simple. It's about keeping your heart clean before God. It's about controlling your tongue. James said that those who could control their tongues were perfect and complete, able to "control themselves in every other way" (Jas. 3:2b NLT). Holiness can be thought of in terms of wholeness—a heart undivided—a mouth aligned with a heart that respects and loves God (see Ps. 86:11).

In Hebrew, the word for *respect* is often translated as "fear." The fear of God is a strong theme throughout the original Hebrew Scriptures. There we find vivid illustrations of the consequences of incurring God's wrath. For example, the consequence of killing a man unjustly was to have that dead man tied to the back of his killer. This was a slow but sure death sentence, because the killer carried the corpse until the bacteria from the decaying body eventually killed him. This paints a picture of what happens when we don't forgive someone—we have to carry the rotting corpse of our resentment and bitterness on our back. We have to drag that person around continuously until the stress eventually kills us. But if we will let it go, God will take care of it for us.

Vengeance Belongs to the Lord

There are two things that God will not share with man. He will not share His glory, and He will not share His vengeance. The Scriptures say, "'Vengeance is Mine, I will repay,' says the Lord" (Rom. 12:19). God means what He says. If we try to get even, God will take His hands off the whole situation, and we'll be on our own, but if instead we pray for those who despitefully use us, our feelings will change and so will our situation. All we need to do is trust God and watch Him work things out.

Genesis chapter 26 tells about a terrible famine. Isaac dug himself a well, only to have his enemies steal it as soon as he found water. This happened several times. Every time Isaac's digging struck water, his enemies rushed in and claimed the well for themselves. This caused Isaac to become angry and bitter toward his enemies. But one day, Isaac began to pray on behalf of his enemies. He prayed for God to bless them. And when Isaac prayed for God to bless his enemies, God caused his empty well to be filled with water. Likewise, if you will let go of your anger and pray a blessing on your enemies, God will cause the emptiness in your life to be filled—He will cause all of your needs to be met. God will produce some real miracles in your life if you will simply let some things go.

God's Word says that if you are at peace with God, He will cause your enemies to be at peace with you (see Prov. 16:7.) Paul encourages us with the words, "If God is for us, who can be against us?" (Rom. 8:31b). The important thing is to put God first—above your offenses, above your hurts, above those who have hurt you. Put God on top and everything else will fall into place.

The Lord is near the brokenhearted; if you call on Him, He will bind up your wounds. If you will forgive others, the Lord will wrap His nail-scarred hands around your heart and take the pain away. The memories may remain, but the pain will be gone. Unforgiveness causes a wound to fester, but when you forgive, the blood of Jesus is like a disinfectant that begins to clean out the wound and will bring healing into your life.

Love Me True

Finally, all of you be of one mind, having compassion
for one another; love as brothers, be tenderhearted, be
courteous; not returning evil for evil or reviling for reviling, but on the contrary blessing, knowing that you
were called to this, that you may inherit a blessing.

1 PETER 3:8-9

There is something about love that strengthens us in
unique ways. Whether you are single or married, God wants
you to develop loving relationships. Those relationships, if
grounded in the love of God, will be a source of peace, health,
and long life. Even if you are single and have no prospect for
marriage, if you get involved in your church, you will experience loving relationships that will become a source of strength
to you. If you are married, get involved in your local church,
and you will find the support you need to sustain a strong, loving relationship within your marriage.

God's Word is packed full of instructions about how to
develop loving relationships in our lives. The Lord knows

that without love, we will fail. We must learn to operate in His divine love in all areas of our lives, with all people, and in every kind of relationship. As Peter says in the verses above, we are to have compassion for one another, be tenderhearted toward one another, and be courteous to each other. God wants us to grow up and become loving members within His Body not only so we can be blessed, but so we can bless others also.

One Body

One of our most important love relationships is the one we have with our spouse, or future spouse. Even if you are not in a marriage relationship, or courting someone, or engaged to someone you hope to marry, someday you probably will be. There are some simple but very important lessons the Bible has to teach us about preparing ourselves for the significant, life-long relationship of marriage. If you are longing for an exceptional marriage relationship, or hoping someday to be married, it is never too early—or too late—to learn those biblical basics about relating lovingly to your loved one.

There are five basic principles I want to share that will help equip you to build loving, lasting relationships in your life. Whether you are single or whether you are married, if you practice these five principles, you will succeed in building loving relationships that will be a source of joy and strength all the days of your life.

Submit Yourself to One Another

Foremost, the Bible tells us to "submit to one another out of reverence for Christ" (Eph. 5:21 NLT). God begins the whole process of teaching about marriage by saying, "be submitted to one another." In other words, no one should be "lording it over" anyone else. We all, husbands included, are submitted to each other. Loving marriage relationships are all about collaboration and teamwork.

> *The fullness of joy God has for us is experienced through living a life of giving, not a life of receiving.*

Unfortunately, because we are self-centered by nature, the tendency for most of us is to be controllers instead of submitters, or takers more so than givers. God's best hope for us is that we will learn to forget about ourselves and prefer one another, or submit ourselves to each other, as givers who are motivated by the love of Christ. We will never experience the kind of joy God has for us until we learn to give selflessly.

The fullness of joy God has for us is experienced through living a life of giving, not a life of receiving. Amazingly, no matter how much we give we will always end up being blessed. Givers are the ones who reap the most rewards in all sorts of tangible and intangible ways. It doesn't take long to learn that in the Kingdom of God, living is all about giving.

In the context of marriage, God's plan is for the husband to be so giving to his wife that she cannot resist his love, and for the wife to be so giving to her husband that he cannot resist her love. And maybe that is why we cannot resist God's love, because He is always coming up with new ways to bless us and show us His infinite generosity, whether through a spectacular sunset or a financial miracle. Whatever the case, we can never outgive God.

God's goodness to us is so great that it moves us to be forever committed to Him. That is how we should be toward our spouses—we should treat our mates with such goodness that he or she is forever committed to us. My wife is so giving and so loving to me that there is nothing I wouldn't do for her. That's God's plan. God's will is that we become so giving toward each other that we cannot resist one another.

Paul said that husbands ought to love their wives as their own bodies (see Eph. 5:25), and that he who loves his wife loves himself (see Eph. 5:28). The Bible tells us that if we are married, our bodies do not belong to us, but to our spouses (see 1 Cor. 7:4). It's all really about an attitude of being a giver. It's about meeting the other person's needs and being unselfish. Building loving relationships always requires that we lay down our lives in a sacrificial way.

Building loving relationships always requires that we lay down our lives in a sacrificial way.

Paul told Timothy that in the last days times would be very difficult. He said that people would become more and more self-centered and their love for one another would grow colder and colder (see 2 Tim. 3:1-4). This could not be made any more evident than it is by the abuse we see today in families and in marriage relationships. As people grow more and more selfish, rates of abuse, neglect, and divorce continue to rise.

Our sin nature pushes us all to be selfish. But now that we have given our lives to Jesus, He wants us to be givers. If we are going to build loving relationships, whether we are single or married, then we must learn to become givers in those relationships, not takers. We must stop thinking exclusively about ourselves and learn to give. A special gift or spontaneous kindness is always a welcome surprise. Every now and then we should go out of our way to do something special and be a blessing to those we love, and even to friends and acquaintances. Love is about looking for new, creative ways to meet another person's needs.

Make Decisions Together

Unfortunately, many men have a tendency to say things like, "Well, I'm the head of this house, and so we're just going to do it my way." Such an authoritarian attitude is not scriptural. God told us to be submitted to one another. We are to be of one mind (see 2 Cor. 13:11) and make decisions together. Anytime you are in a loving relationship with somebody, you will not make important decisions by yourself. If you do, you are saying that the other person is not important or worthy. Excluding your spouse from the decision-making process makes him or her feel unimportant, insecure, and unloved. This is why couples should make all major decisions together.

Every husband needs to know that God has given every *wife* the gift of discernment. Notice that I didn't say every *woman*. God gives every wife the gift of discernment. I can't explain it, but my wife can see things I can't see. The Bible says that God has wisdom locked up inside her. As long as you are making decisions together, you've got all that discernment working on your behalf. If you're making decisions separately, it's only a matter of time before your relationship falls apart. Sadly, when people make decisions separately, it's generally because they are unable to trust each other.

We live in a world today where trust is hard to find. Husbands and wives live in the same house with separate bank accounts because they don't trust each other. The pressures of society are so great, the distractions are so many, and the options seem so unlimited, that we don't see how or why we should fully trust anyone. Two people can be married and live two totally separate lives. They are roommates rather than helpmates. God desires that we be of one flesh, with one vision. Far too often, however, spouses have two separate visions, which results in *di*-vision.

If you are a single woman seeking a husband, it is important that you look for a man who is secure enough within himself not to feel the need to make all of the decisions alone. Seek out a man who will nourish you and cherish you enough to share the decision-making process. Some men are simply bullheaded; they think they've got to make all the decisions. But when God put man in the garden, He said, "Work the garden. Cultivate the garden. Bring out the best in the garden." You will want to spend your life with somebody who brings out the best in you. If you find that he's always snapping at you and talking down to you, you better walk away before it's too late.

A man who cultivates his garden properly will always have a radiant wife and successful children.

The man is supposed to bring out the best in his garden—his family. If a husband nourishes his wife properly, she will grow. If he encourages his children as he should, they will flourish. A man who cultivates his garden properly will always have a radiant wife and successful children. However, if he talks down to them, or is negative to them, they will wither.

Let me tell you, fellows, if your wife doesn't look better after you married her than before you married her, you are doing something wrong. Your wife is a product of the way you care for her and the way you nurture her. A woman will fall deeply in love with a man who will nourish, cherish, and cultivate her. Make no mistake about it, a woman in love is radiant and will be your glory (see 1 Cor. 11:7) to the extent that you cherish and nurture her.

Be Adaptable

Adaptability may sound like a trait you would look for in a job candidate, but it is really a characteristic of love. People who are rigid, or who always insist on having things their way, have serious pride and selfishness issues. An inflexible person is oppressive and no fun to be around. Obstinate people are unloving, self-centered, and spiritually immature, and certainly not in the business of spreading God's joy. If you are going to build a loving and joy-filled relationship, you have to be flexible.

Simple reality says that there will be times in any relationship—and especially a love relationship—when you won't get your way. Occasions will arise where you will have to make some huge concessions. That's what maturity in a relationship is all about—making concessions. If you want to have peace in your home and build a lasting, loving relationship, you will have to be adaptable and make some compromises. The Bible says a house divided cannot stand (see Lk. 11:17). For that reason alone we must be flexible, just so that we can have peace in our homes.

Jesus said, "Blessed are the peacemakers, for they shall be called sons of God" (Mt. 5:9). Peacemakers are adaptable and flexible. Peacemakers are humble. Peacemakers are forgiving. When Paul said that we were to be subject to one another, he was really saying that we've got to be adaptable. When we adapt to the needs of our spouse, we are building a loving relationship.

Submission does not mean allowing ourselves to become doormats. Submission means learning to prefer one another in love—to be of service to each other. There is nothing vague about God's style of leadership. Jesus was the ultimate servant. He told us to submit ourselves to one another—to serve each other, prefer one another, and to adapt. Godly leadership is servant leadership. Godliness is about submitting to one another in love.

Support One Another

It may seem self-evident that in loving relationships we must support one another, but too often couples are in competition with each other, or subconsciously trying to sabotage the other in order to prove some point. The longer we are married, the more we seem to take one another for granted, but it is so important to remember that we all need encouragement and praise. We all need to be supported and lifted up by what should be our biggest, one-person fan club—our spouse.

One of the most important things we can do to strengthen our marriage relationships—or any relationship for that matter—is to show unfailing, unconditional, unwavering support. Any time we show support for each other, it makes the entire relationship stronger. The enemy is always trying to erode our support base, silence our promoters, and separate us from the encouragement we so desperately need, so that he can weaken and destroy us.

There is something about encouragement and support that strengthens and helps us to build stronger love relationships. Spouses become insecure when they don't feel supported. If your spouse is insecure, somewhere along the line he or she has not felt your support. It is God's desire that we be such a source of confidence and cheer to our spouses that they feel secure. When I call my wife during the day and tell her she's beautiful, all I'm doing is building security, and security is irresistible.

You know that a relationship is healthy when both sides feel love and support. If you are in a dating relationship and you don't feel encouraged and supported, you need to evaluate your future with that person. Your relationships in life will either strengthen you or weaken you, depending on the nature and character of the other person. This is especially true with regard to the person you choose to marry. There is nothing worse than being in a relationship with someone who does not support you. If you are single and in a relationship that does not strengthen you, you are probably in a dead-end relationship and need to walk away. Look for a relationship with someone who will support you. A supportive relationship will strengthen you in a whole new way.

Sadly, we live in a world that is always trying to bring us down. Not only that, but people are insecure by nature. Any time you neglect or refuse to meet the emotional needs of your loved one, you can be certain that resentment will begin to creep in. If you don't properly support those you love, tension will develop. But whenever we build one another up, we are building security and investing in a more loving relationship. Couples who build a strong framework of mutual support establish an impenetrable relationship that will withstand the tests of time.

Communicate Your Needs

One mistake many of us make is assuming that because someone loves us, he or she automatically knows what we need. Even worse is when we assume that we know what our loved ones need, when in truth we have no idea because we have never asked. Communicating our needs to one another is vital to the health and survival of any relationship, but particularly marriage. We need to be listened to, encouraged, and touched, and so does our spouse. The best way to communicate about these things is to ask questions and then be open to learning how best to love one another. In order to build healthy relationships we must learn how each other hears love.

Simply put, when a relationship is in trouble, it is because someone's needs are not being met. When a marriage is in trouble, it is because somebody is not paying attention. We must learn how those we love *hear* love. Sometimes we must be willing to sit down and tell our loved one how *we* hear love—we have to teach people what we need.

Men especially seem to clam up and not communicate their needs, usually because of pride. It takes humility to open up and be candid. But we need to humble ourselves and say, "Baby, this is what I need." We need to be transparent and communicate how we hear love.

God's plan is for each of us to find the person of our dreams and live happily ever after. Unfortunately, many of us are so unhealthy that when we find the person of our dreams, we end up driving him or her away. We ruin our chances for a loving relationship simply because we don't know what one looks like, or how to communicate what we need.

If you are single today, God wants you to grow. He wants you to change. God's plan is for you to find somebody in church—not in a bar somewhere—who shares goals and dreams, and with whom you can build a loving relationship. God never intended for you to grow old by yourself.

The Power of Commitment

As Christians, our primary and strongest commitment must be to the Lord. If we are committed to the Lord first and foremost, then we will be able to outlast any storm that comes against either us or our marriage. That is why shacking up never works, because your commitment level isn't deep enough. If you are living with someone and don't like what you see, you just take a hike; but when you're married and committed, you stick it out and make it work.

If you are married to someone who is not your best friend, that mentality has to change. You've got to talk to your spouse as if he or she is your best friend, because, ultimately, that is true. Your spouse is (or should be) the best friend you will ever have in this world. You've got to build that person up as if you are his or her biggest fan, because you will reap what you sow. At the same time, your spouse should be your biggest fan. A marriage relationship survives and thrives on unselfish giving. If there is a problem in a relationship, the solution starts with you. Pray for God to change you, because changing the nature of your relationships starts when you change, not the when others do.

Making someone feel loved and supported unlocks that person's potential. I remember when I first met Michele. She was 32 years old and had never had a steady boyfriend in her life. The moment I saw her I said to myself, "Man, there's nothing but potential here. Look at what this girl has to offer." Nobody else could see that, and I'm glad. Because of my love for her, because of my nourishing her, she has flourished. She has blossomed and grown in tremendous ways. It just took someone committed to seeing that potential. When you love somebody with that kind of love, it draws out his or her potential.

We have to be committed to the potential hidden inside each other, and in our relationships. No matter how strong our relationships, there is a level of love many of us have yet to experience. If we are going to have the kind of loving relationships that God has intended for us to have, we have to make the changes needed to get to where God wants us to go.

CHAPTER TEN

Fools for Love

Then the LORD God said, "It is not good for the man to be alone; I will make him a helper suitable for him."

GENESIS 2:18 NASB

We're born alone, we live alone, we die alone. Only through our love and friendship can we create the illusion for the moment that we're not alone.

ORSON WELLES
QUOTED IN HENRY JAGLOM, *SOMEONE TO LOVE* (1985)

Loneliness is one of the most devastating forces at work in the earth. It opens the human heart up to all sorts of invasion from depression to indiscretion to destructive antisocial behavior. That is why God said, "It is not good that man should be alone" (Gen. 2:18). He didn't say it was not good for a man or a woman to be single; He said it was not good for them to be alone. God knows we need others. He created us to thrive in fellowship and to be strengthened in healthy, loving relationships.

Unfortunately, in our modern society, and because of our fast-paced, technology-driven lifestyles, we have become increasingly isolated from one another. It may seem as though we are more connected than ever before, but we are actually more disconnected. We spend more time facing a television screen or hand-held monitor than we do other people. Most of us today have almost forgotten the art of deep sharing and intimate conversation, not only with other people, but with the Lord as well. Who can sit still in our world of distractions long enough to listen?

We need to relearn the sacred art of intimacy—or "into me see"—with one another, with ourselves, and with God.

This artificial sense of connection we have created for ourselves actually has led us to even more isolation and even fewer sincere relationships than ever before. We need to relearn the sacred art of intimacy—or "into me see"—with one another, with ourselves, and with God. It is time to stop and look deeply once again into the hearts of those around us. Even more, we need to understand again the depths of what it means to know God. Only then will we feel truly connected and begin to address the loneliness that is sweeping the world.

Everybody Needs Somebody

Loneliness will steal a person's hope for the future. The pain of loneliness can become so great in people's lives at times that they long for death rather than life. Loneliness is subtle and insidious. It sneaks in slowly, and takes over every part of a person's being. Whether you live alone or with a family of ten, you are vulnerable to its effects. It's not a matter of being single or married. Anyone who is married will tell you that loneliness can be as pervasive in a marriage relationship as it is outside of one. No matter who we are, we will struggle with loneliness at one time or another.

Even Jesus struggled with loneliness. When He went into the garden to pray the night before He was crucified, He asked His disciples to stay awake and pray with Him. On the very night He was betrayed, Jesus asked His friends for prayer and moral support, but they fell asleep instead, and virtually abandoned Him. Jesus, then, experienced firsthand the pain of being alone. It wasn't about Him being single; it was about being alone. The famed Mother Teresa wrote this moving passage:

> Jesus himself experienced this loneliness. He came amongst his own and his own received him not, and it hurt him then and it has kept on hurting him. The same hunger, the same loneliness, the same having no one to be accepted by and to be loved and wanted by. Every human being in that

case resembles Christ in his loneliness; and that is
the hardest part, that's real hunger.
"Imitation of Christ," *A Gift for God* (1975)

No matter who we are, we all need to be around people
who care about us. I learned a few years ago that it's better
not to travel alone. It's not good to be on the road by yourself
for long periods of time. Loneliness can mess with your mind.
Anytime we are isolated, or spend too much time alone, eventually our minds will start doing crazy things. Isolation makes
our minds play tricks on us. The great majority of people who
"lose their minds," as well as control of their lives, are people
who crack under the pain and isolation of loneliness. Could
there be any worse feeling than living life thinking that you are
all alone? There is an ache on the inside of us that almost never
goes away—an ache caused by the desperate need shared by
every single human being - to be loved and to share life with
another person.

The Dangers of Solitude

Loneliness is one of the most painful heartaches in life. It
is so unbearable that even Christians often will keep company
with those they shouldn't in order to avoid feeling lonely even
for a little while. It is dangerously easy for any of us to find
ourselves looking for love in all the wrong places simply because we are lonely. Loneliness can cause you to go out with
someone you shouldn't go out with and marry someone you

shouldn't marry. If you listen too long to its words of despair, loneliness will cause you to get your priorities out of order.

Scripture tells us that we are not to be unequally yoked (see 2 Cor. 6:14). Light and darkness don't mix, and bad company corrupts good morals. But sometimes, when our pain is too great, we don't even care what God's Word says. We may agree with what the Bible says, but, left alone long enough, we will start to do stupid and foolish things. In our attempts to sedate the pain of our loneliness, our minds will fall prey to hellish thoughts. Isolation can lead us to think and do the craziest things. Some people are so lonely that they will do anything for anyone who shows them the least bit of attention.

If you maintain a right attitude like the apostle Paul, however, you will be so busy working for God that you won't have time to get into a mess. One thing you will discover, if you haven't already, is that because you are now a believer in the Lord Jesus Christ, sin can never satisfy you again. It may have been fun at one time, but now if you do something you shouldn't do, you want to kick yourself for a month.

All You Need Is Love

Our need for love is so great that we will make fools out of ourselves just to win someone's love. The moment somebody says, "I love you," we are drawn to them like flies to honey. Whether we want to admit it or not, every single one of us is needy. That is why God told us that if we would seek first His Kingdom and His righteousness, everything we needed would be given to us (see Mt. 6:33). He promised never to leave us or forsake us (see Heb. 13:5). And He tells us that He is the friend who sticks closer than a brother (see Prov. 18:24). But sometimes our soul cries out to be physically touched.

Have you heard the story about the little girl who was asleep in her bedroom when a storm came up? The thunder rolled and the lightening cracked, and she became afraid. She got out of her bed and ran down the hall into her parents' room. Her dad said, "Honey, what's wrong?" She said, "Daddy, I'm scared. I want to get in bed with you."

Her father looked at her and said, "But Honey, you know Jesus is always there with you. He'll never leave you. He's always right there to protect you."

And the little girl said, "Yes, Daddy, I know He's there—but sometimes I need someone with skin on to hold me."

Sometimes we all need somebody with skin on to hold us. We need somebody we can see and hear and touch to hold our hand or give us a hug.

Jesus said, "The thief comes only to steal and kill and destroy; I came that they may have life, and have it abundantly" (Jn. 10:10 NASB). We all have a spiritual enemy that will do everything he can to steal our joy and happiness. One of the ways he does this is through our loneliness. That is why we must make up our minds not to give the enemy a foothold. We must come to a firm resolve not to allow ourselves to fall into the loneliness cycle.

Sometimes we all need somebody with skin on to hold us.

Jesus came to redeem us from the curse of loneliness. He wants you to live a love-filled, joy-filled, fulfilled life. If you let loneliness control your life, the enemy will steal your destiny. He will use your loneliness to draw you to people you shouldn't hang around with, and even possibly sleep with somebody you have no intention of marrying. With loneliness driving everything you do, you will not fulfill your purpose or destiny in life.

Fellowship vs. Relationship

If you are struggling with loneliness, check your social thermometer; are you building loving relationships? The Bible says that if you want friends, you have to show yourself friendly (see Prov. 18:24). But don't confuse fellowship with relationship. Just being with people doesn't solve the loneliness problem. You have to interact. You have to connect. You have to be a part of their life. We can have fellowship with people we don't know, but have relationships with people means being able to call them on the phone, have them over for dinner, or do something fun with them. Fellowship alone will never solve the loneliness problem; only the building of stable, loving relationships will do that.

This concept can prove true in your own household. Although you share the same roof, you might not be building quality relationships with the people you live with. Are you hanging out together, or are you complete strangers who pass in the hallway on your way to your own separate activities? Even married, you can be very lonely if you never take the time to talk. You can become more like roommates than helpmates. You get up and leave the house at different times. You come home at different times. You never eat together. You have separate bank accounts. You go out often in the evenings, but rarely together. The next thing you know, you're taking separate vacations. And then you wonder why you are lonely.

If you are married but are not interacting with each other, making decisions together, praying together, or having fun with one another, then you are not building intimacy. Unless the two of you become best friends, you will end up as two lonely people who happen to share the same roof. Loneliness issues will eat you alive.

It is a known fact that men and women experience relationship issues differently. Men are notoriously poor communicators. Too often it happens with men that once they get married, settled in, and comfortable, they start neglecting their wives. Interestingly, however, men suffer from loneliness more than women do. In fact, the person in our society today most likely to commit suicide is a middle-aged white man, the loneliest member of society due to a common inability to communicate and build healthy relationships. Men believe that they don't have the same social needs as women. They believe they can get married, go to work, come home, eat supper, and sit down in front of the TV set from now until Jesus comes, and they'll be fine. But they're wrong; too often, dead wrong.

There is no question that some people struggle with loneliness more than others do. If both of your parents worked and left you alone, you probably struggle with loneliness issues today. If you were uprooted as a child, going from one school to the next, you probably struggle with loneliness issues. Some people sit at home and drink, not because they like alcohol, but because they're lonely, and drinking is the only way they know how to cope. If you grew up in a dysfunctional family, or suffered divorce, or the death of a loved one, then you probably struggle with loneliness issues. You need to know, however, that if Jesus is Lord of your life, you are no longer a victim. You are a new creation in Christ in the process of overcoming your past—and loneliness is no match for that new creature.

Waiting on God

When we are walking with the Lord, there will be times when He leads us into seasons of solitude. During these times, we learn to wait on God and trust that He is working on our behalf. Loneliness can be useful when it causes us to put the Lord first and to rely on Him for direction and companionship. God used a period of loneliness in my own life to bring me closer to Him. He had to lead me away from the distraction of people and get me off by myself so He could talk to me. Sometimes that is the only way we will stop and listen to His "still, small voice."

If you find yourself in a lonely time, use it as an opportunity to draw near to God. Learn to wait on the Lord so that your strength is renewed (see Is. 40:31.) As Christians, growing up spiritually requires us to make the most of every opportunity. We can learn to use times of solitude to our benefit. We can pray more, wait on the Lord, and practice submitting everything to God. The Lord wants us to look to Him for everything in our lives. Only Jesus can fill our emptiness. Only the Lord of our salvation can fill the loneliness we all struggle with.

Jesus said, "Whoever desires to save his life will lose it, but whoever loses his life for My sake will find it" (Mt. 16:25). In other words, forget about your loneliness. Stop focusing on yourself. Quit getting so hung up on your depression. If you focus on the Lord and serve Him with all your heart, He will bring you whatever you need for a full and abundant life.

Look for Love in the Right Places

Do you remember the song, *Looking for Love in All the Wrong Places?* When I look back over my life, I see where I made a lot of mistakes, simply as a result of loneliness. I have learned how important it is to break the patterns of isolation that can so easily develop in our lives. There are simple steps we can take to avoid the loneliness that causes us to do things we will later regret. For example, if you live alone, you might consider getting a pet, or a roommate, or starting your own home group. Get to know your neighbors; get involved in your church; be active in your community. There may be times where you will have to go alone to the garden to pray, but that should not be how you live every day of your life.

If you are single and looking for love, you have to be careful that you are not looking in the wrong places. Don't fall for someone who isn't serving the Lord or you will have problems in the long run. God said, "Delight yourself in the Lord; and He will give you the desires of your heart" (Ps. 37:4 NASB). It might not be easy to find somebody who is committed to the Lord the way you are, but if you find somebody who loves God more than who loves you, you will have found somebody who will stick with you when the going gets tough.

God said that it is not good for man to be alone. Whether you are single or married, you can surround yourself with healthy relationships. Jesus gave us a beautiful example of how to be single and fulfilled. Jesus surrounded Himself with a number of vibrant relationships in His life. He rarely traveled by Himself. He rarely ate alone. The only time we see Jesus alone was when He went off to pray. Like Jesus, when we go to seek God, it is usually best to go by ourselves, but even then we are not truly alone.

Every human being needs a friend to talk to. We all need somebody we can call and say, "Let's go get a cup of coffee," or, "Let's go to a movie." That is why, if you are married, your spouse ought to be your best friend. If you are not married and don't have any friends, you need to start praying for some. Pray for God to bring you good friends—righteous friends. Ask Him to show you how to be friendly, so that you can reap a harvest of friends.

Never Lonely Again

Sometimes Christians can feel lonelier after they come to the Lord than they felt before they were saved. After they start walking in the knowledge of God, they don't want to hang around the same people or go to the same places anymore.

They might experience a time of aloneness that they aren't used to. I wish I could tell you that after you give your life to the Lord, you won't struggle with feelings of isolation, but I can't. What I can tell you is that there is One who is touched with all the feelings of our infirmities. He feels what you feel. When Jesus was arrested and taken away to be crucified, all of His friends and colleagues walked away from Him. Jesus understands loneliness.

Jesus understands loneliness.

You may feel alone today, but you need to know that you are not in this world alone. The enemy wants you to feel as though God has forgotten all about you. He wants you to feel as though God doesn't care about you. He wants you to lose sight of your destiny and your purpose for living. You may feel lonely, but you are never alone. The Lord is always with you, walking right beside you. Whether you are climbing a mountain or walking down in the valley, wherever you are right now, the Lord is with you.

LOVE MATTERS

❧

CHAPTER ELEVEN

Love and Warfare

> A new commandment I give to you, that you love one another; as I have loved you, that you also love one another. By this all will know that you are My disciples, if you have love for one another.

JOHN 13:34-35

It's not surprising that there is such unrest and despair in the world today. After all, we are living in the last days that Paul warned Timothy about. Paul wrote that people would be unloving and unforgiving, and that their love for one another would grow cold (see 2 Tim. 3:3.) But love is just as powerful today as it has ever been. In fact, as the world grows darker, God's love shines brighter. There is no greater force for good, no better weapon for overcoming evil, and nothing more effective in bringing healing and hope than the love of God.

Our world would be a different place if God's people would learn to walk in love. If Christians learned to demonstrate love in every situation, miracles would be commonplace, and the knowledge of God would cover the earth as the waters cover the sea (see Is. 11:9.) But walking in love sometimes poses more of a challenge than taking down a giant. It requires a different kind of courage and boldness. Walking in love is a discipline that will test every fiber of our being. Our natural man seems to fight every turn we take for love, while the enemy is busy making the road as curvy as possible.

But if we are going to fulfill God's best potential for our lives, we've got to put our love into four-wheel drive. We've got to learn to love people who are not loving toward us. We'll have to learn to crucify our flesh. The truth of the matter is that love is the only real weapon we have to overcome the forces working against us in this world. If we are to have any victory against the kingdom of darkness, any success at spiritual warfare, we must learn to love with a God-kind of love. That, of course, is the kind of love we have been talking about throughout this book - a love that believes the best about everyone, that overlooks a multitude of sins, that does not get offended, and that always forgives (see 1 Cor. 13:1-8; 1 Pet. 4:8; Eph. 4:32.)

Love and Prayer

Satan's plan is to bring strife, division, and unrest into your life so he can stop you from walking in love. His strategy is to get you so offended when you go to church that you'll stop going. It is not an issue of *whether* you will get offended, but of how many times you will get offended before you leave. The question you must answer is, "Will you walk in love, or will you follow after the flesh?" Will you pray for those you have a problem with, or will you talk badly about them behind their back? Jesus put it this way, "Pray for those who spitefully use you and persecute you" (Mt. 5:44b). He didn't say to talk about them, to inform others about your observations, or even to ignore them. He said to pray for them. Why? Because He knew how the flesh works.

As long as we are walking in love, the enemy cannot stop the blessings of God from overtaking us.

When you begin to pray for people that you are having a problem with, God begins to work on your heart. Perhaps you pray believing that God will miraculously change them, but what He is really doing is performing miraculous "heart surgery" on you. Remember, what you measure out is what will come back to you. That principle works with prayer as well. I discovered long ago that when I pray for the Lord to work on someone's heart—to give that person some grace, and to throw in a dose of humility while He's at it—all I'm doing is moving the Spirit to work those same things out in me. And that's a good thing, because as long as I'm walking in God's love, grace, and humility, the enemy cannot stop me.

This is one of the most important keys we can take hold of if we want victory in this life. As long as we are walking in love, the enemy cannot stop the blessings of God from overtaking us. He cannot stop God's provision, healing, or wisdom from working in our lives. But if we give the enemy a foothold by stepping out of love, by getting offended and refusing to forgive, we allow him to have his way with us. A house divided cannot stand, and the only way to keep our house strongly fortified is by walking in unity and love.

We are one Body, and if we are to take this world for Jesus, we must not strive, bicker, or talk about each other. If we could simply understand that the enemy's plan is to divide us so he can conquer, we wouldn't waste any time rooting the strife and division out of our churches—and out of our lives.

Love at All Times

Most of us think we really have it going on when it comes to our love walk, but how many of us have trouble loving our friends when they hurt us, let alone our enemies? Jesus said, "Love your enemies, bless those who curse you, do good to those who hate you, and pray for those who spitefully use you and persecute you, that you may be sons of your Father in heaven" (Mt. 5:44-45a). Then He added, "For if you love only those who love you, what reward have you?...And if you greet your brethren only, what do you do more than others?" (Mt. 5:46-47).

God intended that our love walk would set us apart from the world. In John 13:35, Jesus said, "By this all will know that you are My disciples, if you have love for another." If we can't even love our friends who offend us, how will the world know that we are His disciples?

The moment we give into an offense, we are walking in enemy territory. If we allow ourselves to become offended, it is only a matter of time until the enemy separates and divides us. When we become offended, we begin to see everything through a filter; we begin looking through the eyes of offense instead of the eyes of mercy.

Remember Jesus' words, "Judge not, that you be not judged" (Mt. 7:1). There is no love in a judgmental attitude. Anytime we find fault or criticize, we are demonstrating our limited capacity to love. Whenever we pass judgment, gossip, or even give a haughty look, we are giving the enemy permission to divide and conquer.

Jesus warned that the enemy would send offenses our way to steal the Word of God out of our hearts. That is why it is so easy to go to church, hear the preaching of the Word, and still become offended over something or someone before we even leave the parking lot. Satan uses every kind of offense to steal the Word so that it can't take root in our lives. The more effective he is at keeping the Word from dwelling richly in our hearts, the more certain he can be that we will not walk the path of love and fulfill our destiny in Christ.

We need to overlook one another's shortcomings, pray for one another, and be a source of encouragement instead of discouragement. This is where most parents miss it in raising their children. When their children disappoint them, rather than being quick to discipline and then show love, they withdraw love, as a form of control. Withdrawal of our love leaves room for all sorts of emotional damage and hurt. When we discipline our children, we let them know that we're not pleased with their behavior, but that we will always love them.

We can never withdraw our love from anyone, not even from our enemies. This is one of the qualities that makes the God-kind of love so distinctive. People around us will fail us sooner or later, especially those we love most. But when people fail, we cannot withdraw our love from them. We have all failed and fallen short of the glory of God, but if we didn't always know that God still loved us, we would be without hope. People close to us need to know that we still love them, even when they fail.

Fervent Love

Peter knew the enemy would try to divide the church, which is why he wrote to us, "Above all, keep fervent in your love for one another, because love covers a multitude of sins" (1 Pet. 4:8). This means, as we have already seen, that when we know somebody has failed, we don't spread that information. There is no need or reason to magnify someone's error. Love always seeks to protect rather than expose.

> ### Love always seeks to protect rather than expose.

When we know that someone has sinned and fallen short, we should do everything we can to restore that person in a spirit of gentleness. Religion demands that people be punished, but love cries out for mercy. Religion throws people away when they fail, but love restores. When we understand the love of God—a love that redeems, restores, and resurrects—we can understand what God's love requires of us. We know there is nothing that can separate us from the love of God (see Rom. 8:39.) God certainly doesn't love us because we deserve it; He loves us because He *is* love.

One of the primary reasons people are unable to love others as themselves is simply because they are unable to love themselves. They live under a cloud of condemnation because they don't fully grasp God's unconditional love for them. People who don't understand the love of God can become legalistic and be as demanding of themselves as they are of others. You will only be able to love others as much as you love yourself. I'm talking about knowing who you are in Christ, and accepting and loving who you are.

There will come a time in your life when you must accept who God created you to be, and embrace who you are in Christ (See Rom. 5:5.) But if there is sin in your life, you will never love and accept yourself as you should. As long as you are content to live with your sin, you are going to be disappointed continually with yourself. If you have made mistakes, run to God and repent; don't run away from Him. Submit yourself to God and He will lift you up (see 1 Pet. 5:6), for when you confess your sins He is faithful to forgive and cleanse you from all unrighteousness (see 1 Jn. 1:9).

God wants to help you. His strength is perfected in your weakness (see 2 Cor. 12:7-9). He did not say He would condemn you as a result of your weaknesses, but show Himself strong in your weakness—make up for your weakness with His strength. Imagine if we had that same attitude toward one another.

Fatherly Love

If you did not grow up knowing the love of an earthly father, then you will probably have a hard time understanding the love of your heavenly Father. I have been told that the identity and self-esteem of a child are determined by the love of an earthly father. If you had an absentee father—perhaps a father who lived in the same house, but wasn't emotionally available or didn't interact in your life—you may have a distorted view of fatherly love.

Jesus said He came to earth to reveal the heart of God the Father. He told His disciples, "He who has seen Me has seen the Father" (Jn. 14:9b). In other words, we can know God's heart toward us because we know how Jesus walked and talked while He was among us. That is why we must study the Word. We must know what God says about us—not what religion says, and not what people say—but what the Word of God says.

> **We must know what God says about us— not what religion says, and not what people say—but what the Word of God says.**

When we look at the story of the prodigal son (see Lk. 15), we see a young man who failed and lost all that he had been given. His life ended up in a pigpen, but that is also where it began again. He came to his senses and returned to his father, who threw his arms around him, put a robe on his back, and a ring on his finger. This story shows us that no matter how badly we fail, our Father in heaven thinks of us that very same way. No matter how far we stray, how much time and money we squander, no matter what we do to our reputation, God will always welcome us home when we return to Him.

That is the difference between a relationship and a religion. When you have a relationship with God as your heavenly Father, you are forever grateful for His love, and therefore able to show compassion to others. Religious people often don't pursue an intimate relationship with God as much as they do a system that validates their own ideas. As a result, they can become proud and judgmental, while all the while God is seeking to work through the hearts of the meek and humble with never-ending tender mercies.

God does not cause bad things to happen to us to teach us a lesson. That is a lie of the enemy.

There are religious people who think God puts sickness on people to teach them a lesson. How many loving parents would put cancer on their children to teach them a lesson? How many loving parents would allow their children to get hit by a car to teach them a lesson? God does not cause bad things to happen to us to teach us a lesson. That is a lie of the enemy. Look up Psalm 103:4 and take some time to meditate on the words "loving-kindness" and "tender-mercies."

Brotherly Love

You can measure your love for the Lord by the way you love people. If you say you love the Lord and hate your brother, you are a liar (see 1 Jn. 1:6). If you choose not to forgive others, you prove that you don't understand God's love. When you are judgmental, you show that you don't understand the redemptive power of God's love and mercy.

There is something inside each of us that compels us to be self-righteous. Every single person has a judgmental streak of some kind. We all tend to be critical when people fail. The truth is that people do things for reasons we can never know, and it is not for us to try and figure them out. We must work to grow to the point where we can say, "I don't agree with them, but I'm going to pray for them. I'm not spreading any information; I'm just going to pray." When we are able to do that, we will know we are making some spiritual progress.

We must avoid religious traps. Be aware that religion is concerned with rules, while Jesus is concerned with people. Religion is concerned with appearances, while Jesus is concerned with the condition of our hearts. Religion is concerned with how people dress, while Jesus is concerned with how people love.

Even though we're supposed to hate sin, we must never give the impression that we hate sinners. It's our job to love people, while it is up to the Lord to convict them of their sin. (see Jn. 16:8.) Our job is to love God with all of our hearts and to love our fellow man. We need to leave the judging up to God.

God is more concerned about the condition of your heart than He is about anything you do or give.

Do you love the Lord with all of your heart? If you do, you will also love others with your whole heart. He doesn't want you preaching about Him unless you love those He loves. He doesn't want you singing about Him unless you know how to love Him in spirit and truth (see Jn. 4:24.) He doesn't want you giving your money unless you are able to love others with a pure heart. If you've got something in your heart toward anyone, leave your money at the altar and go reconcile with your brother before you put it in the offering (see Mt. 5:23-24.) God is more concerned about the condition of your heart than He is about anything you do or give.

Loving God

We all know it's not easy to love folks sometimes. It is easy to love God, however, because He loves us so much and is so good and merciful toward us. But God set it up so that we could only really show our love for Him when we love other people. We can only return His love by loving people no matter what they do. I have observed preachers who say they love God with all of their hearts, yet they have no love for people. It is a difficult thing to preach the truth in love. It is a challenge to preach against sin without condemning people, but you will never reach a group of people by condemning them, only by lifting up the name of Jesus and shedding His love into their lives.

One thing I've noticed over the years is that we all need to be loved in a massive way—and the more baggage we have, the more we need to be loved. But there are some people who have so much baggage in their lives that they continually push people away from them. They go from relationship to relationship, from job to job, and from church to church. The people with the most baggage are the people who need the most love. Sadly, the people who need the most love, and who are hurting the most, are also the people who most often have the tallest walls around them to shut out others. They are depriving themselves of the very thing they need the most.

The plain message of Jesus Christ is that we are to love God with all of our hearts, love our neighbors, and love ourselves. To do this we've got to *sow* love. We need to break down the walls we've put up, and reach out to a hurting world. We need to keep on loving those who have walled themselves in, because love will never fail to break through.

How much do you love the Lord? Jesus asked Peter three times, "Do you love me?" And when Peter answered, "Yes, Lord, I love you," the Lord told him, "Love my sheep" (see Jn. 21:15-17.) You prove your love for the Lord by loving people who don't deserve your love. You prove you belong to Christ when you take somebody to lunch who has hurt you. You prove you're on your way to heaven when you don't allow an offense to dictate your behavior.

Warring Love

The truth about love is that it is down and dirty spiritual warfare. We think of spiritual warfare as defeating the enemy in prayer, but the greatest warfare you'll ever have in this life is to love somebody who doesn't deserve your love. God loved you and me when we didn't deserve it, and He expects us to do the same.

If you need to learn how to love—and that's the majority of us—begin by getting on your face before God and saying, "God, I don't know how to love. Teach me how to forgive. Teach me how to let go of things. Teach me not to be so rigid and so harsh. Teach me not to be so self-righteous." Humble yourself before God and say, "God, I need You to do a work inside of me, because I want to be all that You have called me to be."

Study the nature of God, study the Word of God, and spend time seeking God. The more you do those things, the more you will align your heart with His—and the more His nature will become your nature. The nature of God is to love the unlovable, to help people that don't deserve help, and to bless those that don't deserve to be blessed. Jesus showed compassion to the sinners, but got angry with the religious people. If you're a sinner today, God is for you, not against you. You are exactly the kind of person He is looking to share Himself with and promote. But if you are a proud, self-righteous, religious person, God will oppose you (see Jas. 4:6).

If you can begin to grasp the depth of God's love, then you can begin to receive His love. If you can begin to receive God's love, then you can begin to love yourself. And if you can love yourself, then you can begin to love people the way God does.

LOVE MATTERS

CHAPTER TWELVE

Love Never Looks Back

> Do not remember the former things, Nor consider the things of old.
>
> Behold, I will do a new thing, Now it shall spring forth; Shall you not know it?
>
> I will even make a road in the wilderness And rivers in the desert.
>
> ISAIAH 43:18-19

So much can happen in our lives that leave us with bad memories and regrets. Life has a way of disappointing us. A broken relationship leaves us with painful memories. The death of a loved one fills us with heartache and sorrow. A friend's betrayal, a divorce, a bankruptcy—any of these things can render us brokenhearted and regretful.

As painful as all these things are, however, nothing leaves us with more regrets than our own mistakes. The Bible says we have all sinned and fallen short of the glory of God (see Rom. 3:23). That means we have all made mistakes—and we all will continue to make mistakes. But whatever we do, we cannot allow the regrets of our past to rule our future. We must allow the love of God to restore us and propel us toward greater things.

I want to share with you six tools that I have found valuable in helping people let go of the bad memories and "press toward the goal for the prize of the upward call of God in Christ Jesus" (Phil. 3:14). Each represents a different facet of putting God's love into action in a practical way.

Release the Memories

Love allows us to forgive ourselves. God's love helps us move past our mistakes and let go of the memories that hold us back. Some memories hold us back because they are good—we regret that things aren't the way they used to be. In some cases, we want to go back and relive the past. However, we must believe that God has better things ahead of us. God loves us too much to leave us wallowing in regret of any kind. His Word says that He has a plan for our lives—a hope and a future (see Jer. 29:11). Tomorrow will be better than yesterday, and eternity will be better still. His Word says, "Eye has not seen, nor ear heard, nor have entered into the heart of man the things which God has prepared for those who love Him" (1 Cor. 2:9).

I believe it is human nature to live in the past. For some reason, we are averse to change and therefore hang onto the past no matter how unhealthy or destructive it is to do so. We are fearful of change and tend to hold onto the way things used to be—the way things have always been done. We hang onto to old routines and memories of the "good old days."

Isaiah urged us to quit thinking about the things of the past so that God could do a new thing in each of us. As long as we dwell on the past, we won't be open to seeing the new opportunities God has prepared for us. Live each day with great expectation, and in anticipation of the good things God has planned for you.

> ## *Live each day with great expectation, and in anticipation of the good things God has planned for you.*

We must do as Paul instructed in Philippians 4:8; we must think on "whatever things are true, whatever things are noble, whatever things are just, whatever things are pure, whatever things are lovely, whatever things are of good report." We can all agree that bad memories are not good things. Quit thinking on those bad memories. Think on good stuff. We must change our thinking—be renewed in the spirit of our minds—by getting the Word of God in our hearts (see Eph. 4:23). Begin to think on good things.

Make New Plans

When you are stuck in the past, when you are living in your memories, whether good or bad, you don't make new plans. All you do is get yourself a box of Kleenex and a mirror so you can look into it, see how pitiful your life is, and feel sorry for yourself. You don't make new plans when you're feeling sorry for yourself. You are stuck in a rut of self-pity.

But God says, "I've got a future for you. I've got new plans for you." No matter who you are, what you've done, or what you've been through, God says, "I've got new plans for your life. I'm ready to do a new thing in you." God wants you to step out in faith and change direction if you need to. He wants you to make new plans.

Making new plans requires faith. There is something about making new plans that lets everybody know that you are through living in the past. You've got to come to the point where you trust God enough to let go and move on. You've got to be willing to let Him set a new order to your life.

The apostle Paul knew about regrets. He had been persecuting and killing Christians with a vengeance. It was very apparent that after he gave his life to the Lord, he felt tremendous regret over his past. I know that when I gave my life to the Lord, I looked back over my life, and felt tremendous regret because I had wasted so many years living for myself. It wasn't long, though, before I learned that it doesn't do any good to live in the past. You've got to reach for the promises that God has for your future. Paul understood that he had to get his past behind him if he was going to have a future. He knew that he had to forget what lies behind and reach forward to what lies ahead (see Phil. 3:13.)

When you live with regrets, you give the enemy an opportunity to destroy you. Your spiritual enemy loves to steal your future and destroy your potential by causing you to live in the regrets of your past. But when you make new plans, you are saying, "I'm through with my old self and am becoming a new creation in Christ" (see 2 Cor. 5:17). When you make new plans, you are making a declaration that you are ready for God to do a new thing in your life.

Trust in Jesus

To make new plans, you have to trust in God. You have to put your past on the cross with Jesus. While the enemy wants to hold you in your past, Jesus gave Himself so that you could be free from it. There is power in Jesus' sacrifice to help you start over. We're not talking about religion. We're talking about a relationship with the risen Christ who gave Himself so your past could be washed away forever.

Most of us fear any kind of change. Change means getting out of our comfort zones. The enemy uses this fear of discomfort to keep you from going forward. That's why you must remember that Jesus gave His blood so that you could start over. He gave His blood so that you could be free from your past and all its regrets.

The Bible tells us, "Therefore, if anyone is in Christ, he is a new creation; old things have passed away; behold, all things have become new" (2 Cor. 5:17). No matter who you are or what you have done, Jesus will help you start over. Accept that there are some things in your past that you cannot change. You just have to repent and let them go. You have to shake the dust off of your feet and quit looking back, once and for all.

No matter who you are or what you have done, Jesus will help you start over.

❦

Chapters nine and ten of Hebrews tell us that Jesus is our high priest who took His blood into the Holy of Holies to make the ultimate sacrifice for sin on our behalf. Because of what Jesus has already done, we can boldly come to His throne of grace and receive mercy. We can boldly draw near to His throne—not of judgment, but of mercy and grace.

Therefore, brethren, having boldness to enter the Holiest by the blood of Jesus, by a new and living way which He consecrated for us, through the

> *veil, that is, His flesh, and having a High Priest*
> *over the house of God, let us draw near with a true*
> *heart in full assurance of faith, having our hearts*
> *sprinkled from an evil conscience and our bodies*
> *washed with pure water. Let us hold fast the con-*
> *fession of our hope without wavering, for He who*
> *promised is faithful.*

Hebrews 10:19-23

The blood of Jesus shouts that God is not angry with us, but loves us more than we can comprehend. His greatest desire is for us to put every sin and regret under the blood so that we can put our past behind us once and for all. Why would He go to such great lengths for you to live even one day plagued by guilt or shame? The blood Jesus shed lets us know that we can let go of our regrets and trust God for new beginnings.

Break Free from Condemnation

Paul not only knew about regrets; he also knew about failures. Listen to his candid admission in Romans:

I do not understand what I do. For what I want to do I do not do, but what I hate I do. I know that nothing good lives in me, that is, in my sinful nature. For I have the desire to do what is good, but I cannot carry it out. For what I do is not the good I want to do; no, the evil I do not want to do—this I keep on doing. Now if I do what I do not want to do, it is no longer I who do it, but it is sin living in me that does it.

Romans 7:15, 18-20 NIV

He said, "I want to be good, but sometimes I find myself doing the very evil that I'm against." Have you ever been there in your life? You knew the right thing to do, but you just couldn't seem to keep on doing it. If Paul, the great apostle, struggled with staying on track, and yet did not condemn himself for what he knew was his very nature, how much more should we be free from condemnation? He knew that in his own strength he would continually fail, but by the grace of God and the power of Christ working in him, he would succeed—by grace through faith (see Eph. 2:8).

If your spiritual enemy can cause you to live in guilt, then he can steal your happiness. He can steal your future in Christ. Remember that Jesus took your punishment two thousand years ago! You don't have to punish yourself for your failures. God doesn't want you going on a guilt trip every time you stumble. Anytime you live with guilt in your life, it will cause you to be full of regrets, which will keep you from moving on with God.

Romans 8:1 tells us that there is no condemnation to those who are in Christ—which translates as "no condemning sentence." John reassures us that "If we confess our sins, "He is faithful and just to forgive us our sins and to cleanse us from all unrighteousness" (1 Jn. 1:9).

The problem is that so often we live our lives by feelings rather than by what God's Word says. We confess our sins, but because we don't *feel* forgiven, we start saying to ourselves, "I don't feel like God loves me. I don't feel like God has a plan for my life. I don't feel like God is going to help me." In this regard, how we feel does not matter; what matters is what God says about us in His Word. Which are we going to trust, our feelings, or the Word of God?

You have to know what the Word of God says, and then you have to line up your thoughts and words with what it says. Feelings are too often wrong. The enemy's plan is to bring guilt into your life and make you think that you can't go on. His scheme is to bring the feelings of guilt into your life so you never fulfill your life's purpose.

God has a plan and purpose for your life, and He has already done everything necessary for you to fulfill it.

But the truth is, God has a plan and purpose for your life, and He has already done everything necessary for you to fulfill it. The enemy wants to keep you from your purpose because then he can keep you from touching the lives of others. Your spiritual adversary wants you to think that you're too far gone—that your sin is too great for God to forgive. But that's not true. This is like saying that Jesus' sacrifice was not enough, and that He needs to come back to earth and die on the cross all over again. It is simply not true.

Love at all Times

You will never get your past behind you until you accept the fact that Jesus paid for your sins. And you will never be able to move forward until you forgive others for what they've done to you. This sums up the great commandment, love the Lord with all your hearts, and love your neighbor as yourself (see Mt. 22:37-39). Loving others requires that you forgive them, and loving "as yourself" requires that you also forgive yourself. In order to forgive ourselves, we must put God first, ahead of our feelings, and obey His Word that says that He loves and forgives us. Part of loving God with our whole heart is being responsive to His love for us.

Part of loving God with our whole heart is being responsive to His love for us.

However, the accuser is always there to remind you of your faults and shortcomings. He is always trying to take you captive with feelings of guilt and condemnation. Revelation 12:11 tells us how to deal with our enemy, "They overcame him (the enemy) by the blood of the Lamb and the word of their testimony." You can overcome the enemy's accusations if you open your mouth and change your testimony. You can overcome all your regrets if you choose not to live with guilt. Confess your sins and banish the guilt that came from them.

I can personally say that I have let the Lord down more times than I want to remember. But one thing I do know is that He loves me, so I keep on repenting, and He keeps on forgiving. That's why I can let go of the guilt, because I know who He is and what He has done for me.

Even Peter, the "rock," denied that he knew the Lord on three different occasions. Talk about making a mistake! And we know that Judas betrayed the Lord. Both had tremendous regrets. Both had failed the Lord. Both were sorry for what they had done. But only Peter repented. Judas could have been restored. He could have been forgiven had he simply said, "God, I am sorry. Forgive me of my sin." God would have turned his life around. But he didn't—and his guilt destroyed him.

The enemy's plan is to cause you to go on a guilt trip so that, like Judas, you destroy yourself. Judas could have been restored had he only repented. Restoration is possible for anyone who has failed. God will restore any of us who simply humble ourselves enough to ask Him.

Don't Look Back

Failure is not the end. The Bible says that God's mercies are new every morning (see Lam. 3:22-23.) If you failed Him yesterday, God has a fresh compassion for you today. Isn't that good news? No matter how many times you fail Him today, when you get up tomorrow morning, you have brand new mercies waiting for you.

The Good News of Jesus Christ is about starting over and making a fresh start in your life every day. It's about overcoming all of the obstacles and stumbling blocks that the enemy tries to put in your way. It's about trusting God for new beginnings no matter what has happened to you, or what mistakes you've made.

No matter how many regrets you have from the past, everything is subject to change when you put the Lord first in your life. Maybe you have experienced the worst year of your life. Maybe you have so many regrets that you can't count them all. Maybe your goals and dreams have been shattered, but God wants you to know that you can start over today.

No matter how many mistakes you've made, God's nature is to give you grace and mercy. The Bible says that God is love. He doesn't *have* love—He *is* love—and God is in love with you. He cannot help Himself, because He is love. None of us deserve that love, but that is what grace and mercy are all about. All that is required of you is faith in God—believing that He will do something new in your life.

Once God brought the children of Israel out of Egypt, there was still something inside of them that wanted to go back to their past. This happens all the time today. People give their lives to the Lord and start walking with Him. They experience some victories, just as the children of Israel did, but when the going gets a little rough, they start thinking, "I'm going to go back to my old life, because it wasn't as hard then as it is now." That is nothing but a lie from the enemy.

If you're going to go to the next level, if you're going to go to a new place in God, you've got to quit looking back.

The children of Israel kept remembering all the tasty things of their past. They kept talking about the past because they didn't believe that God had a future for them. But if you're going to go to the next level, if you're going to go to a new place in God, you've got to quit looking back. Egypt is not your inheritance—it's your past. Your sin is your past. Quit looking back. The promised land is ahead of you, so quit looking back. You may be in the wilderness today, but don't look back. You cannot enter your land of promise as long as you are still looking over your shoulder. There is nothing in your past that is worth giving up your future for. As long as you keep looking back, you are going to live with regrets.

We have all heard the story about how God delivered Lot's family from Sodom, the city of sin. He instructed them that as they left their old life behind, they should not look back under any circumstances. God said, "I'm going to bring you out of your trouble, but whatever you do, when I bring you out, don't look back." But Mrs. Lot couldn't keep from looking back. God wanted to take her to a new place, but she had to look back one more time. He wanted to do a new thing in her life, but because she couldn't keep from looking back, she was turned into a pillar of salt.

God has brought you out of your former life, and now, whatever you do, don't look back. Remember Lot's wife. She was on her way to a new beginning and a new future, but for some reason there was still something in her past that she couldn't let go of. So she disobeyed God, looked back, and that mistake destroyed her. Don't let that happen to you. Don't look back one more time—not one more day.

Accept God's grace. Draw on His mercy. Receive His great love for you with a grateful heart. Allow Him to lead you away from your former life and make all things new. Take His hand and follow Him away from your past. Once God brings you out of your trouble, puts your hand to the plow and move forward, never looking back again.

CHAPTER THIRTEEN

Ruled by Love

> But you are a chosen race (**a chosen generation**), a
> royal priesthood, a holy nation, a people for God's own
> possession, so that you may proclaim the excellencies
> of Him who has called you out of darkness into His
> marvelous light; for you once were not a people, but
> now you are the people of God; you had not received
> mercy, but now you have received mercy.
>
> I Peter 2:9-10 NAS (INSERT ADDED)

As we go through life, we don't always achieve our goals;
we experience failures and we make mistakes. There are times
we get down on ourselves for our lack of success or for the
poor decisions we have made. It is only natural for us to begin
doubting ourselves when we endure one failure after another.
The problem comes when we start thinking that failure defines our life. The change from thinking, "I failed," to "I am a
failure," is a very subtle change, but it can have devastating effects. Seeing ourselves as failures can chain us to our past and
lock us into a cycle of defeat and despair. To fail occasionally

is a part of life, but that doesn't mean we *are* failures. God certainly doesn't see us that way. He sees the potential He put inside of us; the seed of greatness that is watered and nurtured by His great love for us.

The Bible says, "As [a man] thinks in his heart, so is he" (Prov. 23:7a). Eventually we all become what we think of ourselves. If you think you're no good, you will live that out. If you think you're nothing but a failure, you will become a failure. That's why it is so important to know what the Bible says about you—not what your mamma said about you, or what society says about you, but what God says about you.

God says that as the people of God, we are a royal priesthood and a holy nation. But when you've been beaten down is when you have to get reprogrammed with the Word of God. You have to know what God says about you. That's why you need go to church, read your Bible, and fellowship with God's people. You need to continually renew your mind to who you are in Christ.

Know Your DNA: *Divine Nature Acquired*

You were created in God's image. You did not evolve from a tadpole or a monkey. God created you in His own image and likeness. Then, when you accepted Jesus as Savior and Lord, you were adopted into His family. You didn't deserve to be adopted, but He loved you and chose you anyway. His mercy said, "Welcome to the family! I'm adopting you!" And now, as a child of God, you are a co-heir with Jesus, "if children, then heirs—heirs of God and joint heirs with Christ" (Rom. 8:17a).

God made each of us different. As new creatures in Christ (see 2 Cor. 5:17), we are not like the rest of the world. And as individual members of the Body, we are each unique. Although we are conformed to the image of Christ (see Rom. 8:29), too often we mistake that conformity for dressing according to a given code, or acting according to a legalistic set of man-made rules.

We need to learn to love ourselves just as we are, because that is who God created us to be.

Society would try to make us believe that we are supposed to look alike, but God made each of us unique for a reason. No two of us are exactly alike, not even twins. And no matter what we look like, or what our culture, race, or background is, we have all been adopted into the family of God. We must learn to love one another, including ourselves, simply because of who we are in Christ. We need to learn to love ourselves just as we are, because that is who God created us to be.

We are not supposed to look, act, or dress the same. Look at creation, the vast variety of species and ecosystems. One of the greatest beauties about God's creation is its diversity. We are all so different, and yet it is this very diversity that makes the body of Christ so beautiful to behold. Even though no two of us are the same, as members of one body we all are righteous before God and can have the mind of Christ, sharing one heart, one mind, and one Spirit.

God created you as unique as your fingerprints for a reason. Only you can do what God has put you on the earth to do! You will touch people that nobody else can touch. You will share His love in a way that could come only through you. You have no competition for being you, and no reason to be envious of anyone else. You can rest in God's love for you, knowing that He created the divine package of your unique being for a special purpose.

Don't Be Deceived

If you come from a family that always puts you down, then you will have a tendency to feel like a failure more than you should. Just because you've had failures doesn't mean you *are* a failure. You may have experienced failure, but if you have learned from your failures, you have been made smarter and stronger because of them. Many people would pay big money to learn some of the lessons you have learned, because your experiences have given you the equivalent of a master's degree in some areas.

I used to let low self-esteem hold me down, but after I came to the Lord and started getting the Word of God inside of me, things began to turn around in my life. With the help of the Holy Spirit and the Word of God, I got my act together. There is no problem, situation, or person that is beyond the grace of God! Everything is just raw clay to the Master Potter—all He sees is your potential.

For better or worse, whatever you constantly hear is what you will eventually believe. That is why it is so important to go to the right church, listen to the right preachers, and be careful about what you feed into your heart through your ears, your eyes and your mind. You've got to be very careful what you listen to, because whatever you hear long enough is eventually what you will believe.

Remember, faith comes by hearing (and hearing, and hearing) the Word of God. If you believe you are a failure, it is only because you have not gotten into the Word and educated yourself about who you are in Christ. You have not heard what God says about you enough to build you up on the inside. Renew you mind. As Paul says, "Be transformed by the renewing of your mind, that you may prove what is that good and acceptable and perfect will of God" (Rom. 12:2).

Know Your Opposition

Your spiritual enemy wants you to get down on yourself. He wants you to think you are unattractive, unintelligent, and inferior. Satan wants you to believe that you are a loser, a person whom no one could possibly love. In truth, the hardest people to love are people who don't like themselves. Don't let the enemy cause you to get down on yourself, because if you buy into his lies, you will fulfill them by becoming unlovable, simply because it is what you believe about yourself.

We all deal with low self-esteem to a certain degree. Every one of us has at one time or another been treated harshly, talked down to, or demoralized. When we are beaten down repeatedly, we tend to create our own protection mechanisms so that nobody can hurt us again. We build walls and isolate us, often withdrawing and becoming somewhat of a loner. Sooner or later, however, we have got to get our acts together and learn to obey God. We need to learn who we are in Christ. It's time to quit listening to the lies of the enemy.

God did not create you to live in failure. He did not create you to be a slave to your past. He created you for victory.

If life has beaten you down and you don't think much of yourself, take heart in the fact that Jesus came to turn your situation around. He came to let you know that you are a somebody and not a nobody. You may feel like a loser, but God says you're a winner in Christ. He said you are a joint heir with His Son. That means that whatever belongs to Him belongs to you.

When you know who you are in Christ, everything can change suddenly. All you have to do is get hold of God's Word and know that God did not create you to live in failure. He did not create you to be a slave to your past. He created you for victory. You don't have to stay stuck in your past. Make up your mind to live for the Lord. Put your shoulders back and know that you are a joint heir with Jesus Christ, the King of Kings and the Lord of Lords.

Be Receptive to Grace

Now that you love the Lord, you have to know that God is on your side. You have to realize that "greater is he that is in you, than he that is in the world" (1 Jn. 4:4b KJV). You can know that you are "His own special people, that you may proclaim the praises of Him who called you out of darkness into His marvelous light" (1 Pet. 2:9b). You are not a grasshopper; you are somebody, a person of worth and value. If you will begin to seek God and get the sin out of your life, He will begin the process of turning your life around.

Get out of the cycle of sin and into the cycle of blessing. Start by putting the Lord first—loving the Lord with all your heart. If you can do that, then loving your neighbor as yourself won't be so difficult. This is the key to turning your life around - love God supremely, love others, and love yourself.

Don't stay stuck in the past. Now that you are a new creature in Christ, you can put your past behind you. You can overcome every giant. You can overcome every rejection. You can overcome all the issues of your past because you are more than a conqueror through Christ Jesus who loves you (see Rom. 8:37).

It is time to let go of your guilt. One of the main reasons people live with guilt is because they go to the Lord, receive forgiveness, and then go right back to doing the same things they did before. And guilt plagues them. It becomes a vicious cycle. You can eliminate the guilt in your life if you will make up your mind to sell out to the Lord and put Him first in everything. Once you know who you are in Christ, you will quit putting yourself down, quit feeling bad about yourself, and quit falling back into the same old sins.

Change Your Words

Jesus told us to be careful of the things we say because our words determine how we come out of our trouble. If you have a rebellious child, be careful what you say about him or her. Don't call your son or daughter a fool, or stupid, because these things have a way of coming to pass. Whatever you speak out will take root and start to grow. Our words are like seeds. Jesus said, "For by your words you will be justified, and by your words you will be condemned" (Mt. 12:37). This means you've got to be careful what you say about your marriage, too. You may not like where you are, but if you can't say something good, you'd better keep your big mouth shut.

Ecclesiastes 10:20 NASB states, "Furthermore, in your bedchamber do not curse a king, and in your sleeping rooms do not curse a rich man, for a bird of the heavens will carry the sound and the winged creature will make the matter known." In other words, everything you say—gossip, murmuring, backbiting, criticism, cursing—will go into the heavens, where a creature will make sure it is exposed in the earth. Whatever you say in private will be exposed to the world.

The very next verse says, "Cast your bread on the surface of the waters, for you will find it after many days" (Eccles. 11:1). At first glance, this verse seems to be talking about sowing and reaping, but the context relates to the things we say in private. We cast our "bread" on the water, and eventually it returns to us. This is a clear warning about the importance of holding our tongue. We need to stop speaking negatively about our children, our spouse, and ourselves.

You frame your world by the words of your mouth. Change what you're saying about yourself and the people around you. How do you want your relationships to look? Do you want peace? Then speak peace over people—and speak peaceably about them. Get into agreement with God's Word and speak out what God says about you and His best hope for the world. God says, "The earth will be filled with the knowledge of the glory of the Lord as the waters cover the sea" (Hab. 2:14), and, "All the earth shall be filled with the glory of the Lord" (Num. 14:21).

Speak Life

You may not feel like it, and you may not look like it, but God says you are royalty. It is your responsibility to say what God says about you, not what society says about you. God's Word says that the "greater one" lives in you. It says you have been adopted into the family of God. Your life will begin to come together when you begin to agree with what God says about you, instead of what people say about you.

When God told Ezekiel to prophesy to the valley of dry bones, He was telling him to speak life to his dead situation. He was telling him to prophesy good things over his bad circumstances because prophecies have a tendency to become self-fulfilling. Speak good things to the bad situation in your life. That's what faith is all about. You don't have much faith if you can't speak good in a bad situation.

Even when you feel things are as bad as they've ever been, you can say, at the very least, that better days are ahead. Jesus told us that if we will change our confession, we can start the process of seeing things turn around. Confessing Jesus as Lord is a start, but remember also that the Bible says that we will overcome by the blood of the Lamb and the word of our testimony (Rev. 12:11).

God created you to walk in victory. He asks you to follow after Him and become someone who "calls things that are not as though they were" (Rom. 4:17b NIV). Your words are like the rudder of a ship or the bit in a horse's mouth (see Jas. 3:4.) The reason you keep going off course is because of your words. A large part of perfecting your love walk is learning to let love rule your tongue.

A large part of perfecting your love walk is learning to let love rule your tongue.

When you confess Jesus as the Lord of your life, you become the righteousness of God (see 2 Cor. 5:21), which means that you are in right standing with God. You are clothed in His righteousness. This has nothing to do with religion, but with the blood of Jesus that covers our sin and takes away our guilt and shame.

You shouldn't put yourself down because of what God has done for you. God says you are the head and not the tail (see Deut. 28:13) He says that you are more than a conqueror (see Rom. 8:37.) Why do we waste so much time arguing with God about how unworthy, unable, or inferior we feel? God wants us to get our thinking in alignment with His. If God says you are more than a conqueror, and that you are royalty, righteous, and holy, then you need not have a low opinion of yourself.

Stop talking about all the things you can't do, and start saying, "I can do all things through Christ who strengthens me" (Phil. 4:13). Change your words, because your future is at stake. Whatever you say is going to come back to you. Stop saying, "I can't make it," and start saying, "I'm going somewhere." Things may not look good today. You may feel lost in the wilderness, you may feel as if you are wandering aimlessly, but if you keep your heart, mind, and mouth anchored in love, you will be well on your way to taking ownership of the land God has promised you.

Play to an Audience of One

God is looking for those who will show themselves faithful (see 2 Chron. 16:9). Are you speaking faith out of your mouth? If you are in a tough situation and things look difficult, do you brag on God, or do you magnify the enemy?

Don't let other people's opinions get stuck in your head. You already know that it is impossible to please all the people all the time. You can do everything right and still not please some people. One day they might love you, and the next day they won't even take your phone call. Stop trying to please people and focus instead on being a God-pleaser.

Your Inner Lion

Now that you love the Lord, there is a lion inside you, a champion eager to be released. Change the words of your mouth. Know who you are in Christ. You have been made the righteousness of God Himself. He created you to love, not hate; to conquer, not to be defeated. You have got to see yourself through the eyes of God.

And because your past has been a tremendous teacher, you won't make the same mistakes this year that you made last year. You are going to press toward the mark of the high calling in Christ (see Phil. 3:12-14.) It's time to change your words. It's time to say, "No weapon formed against me shall prosper. If God be for me, who can be against me? I am the righteousness of God through the blood of Jesus Christ!"

Even if you have had more failures than you can count, God doesn't hold your failures against you. God does not see your filthy rags. All He sees is His righteousness covering you. He came to redeem, restore, and resurrect your life. If you've got the right attitude—if you will begin to love yourself as much as God does, and love others as you do yourself—then you will have the faith to ask and see God do impossible things.

CHAPTER FOURTEEN

༽Წ

Living under Love

He chose us in Him before the foundation of the world, that we should be holy and without blame before Him in love, having predestined us to adoption as sons by Jesus Christ to Himself, according to the good pleasure of His will, to the praise of the glory of His grace, by which He made us accepted in the Beloved.

EPHESIANS 1:4-6

Whether or not they put their hope in Christ, every person on the planet wants a better life. As believers, we know that Jesus came that we would have a more abundant life. We know that God wants us to use our life for His Kingdom. He wants us to live for something beyond just our job and our own household. God has a purpose for our lives greater than making a living, raising children, and retiring in comfort. His purpose is to use us in His kingdom so that we can experience a richer and deeper fulfillment in this life.

Because every one of us is looking for a better quality of life, many of us fall into every imaginable sin looking for that kind of satisfaction. Too many seek contentment through other people; they either look for love in the wrong places, or look for the wrong kind of love.

Some people search for contentment in religion. Actually, they are searching for God's love in religious ways, but they won't find it until they understand that it's not about religion, but about relationship. We have learned that love is something made alive when our hearts are intimately connected to God and to each other. The Word of God has taught us that without love, we are nothing, and that without love our faith is dead. Without love, we cannot truly call ourselves children of God.

Our Life in Christ

Whenever someone gives his or her life to the Lord Jesus Christ, it is almost always out of a desire for a better life than he or she has experienced in the world. If people simply would learn to sit down and objectively evaluate the risks and rewards of heaven versus hell—of life in Christ versus life without, or of the goodness of God versus the fickleness of people in this world—they would conclude that it was a good decision to give their lives to Jesus Christ. But most of us don't give our lives to the Lord until we are in a mess, or until we don't have any place else to turn.

The bottom line is that we all want a better quality of life. When we give our lives to the Lord, it is because we want the joy, peace, and love that we haven't found in the world. Jesus said, "I have come that they may have life, and that they may have it more abundantly" (Jn. 10:10b). Abundant living certainly relates to quality of life, and the only way we can live abundantly is by walking with the Lord faithfully every single day.

> ## The only way we can live abundantly is by walking with the Lord faithfully every single day.

God created you to have a good life. He created you to have big dreams and visions, and to be fulfilled and blessed. God wants you to know that if you walk with Him every single day, you will have a better life. Don't become disillusioned if things don't turn around for you overnight. Growth and success are a process that takes more time than that!

God expects you to grow. He expects you to study to show yourself approved. If you don't have a personal growth program, you will stagnate and probably even slip backwards. You can be in church every Sunday and Wednesday, yet if you do not apply yourself, you will not grow. Growth is not automatic. That is why you've got to have a plan.

Are You Growing?

Successful people are always growing. If you are not growing, you probably are not experiencing much success. Unfortunately, many Christians do not see their lives getting better day by day because they don't have a growth plan. Many Christians simply don't apply themselves. They fall into negative patterns and live roller-coaster lives. Some even fall into destructive behavior. That is why God wants you to get into His Word. The power for grow is found in the Word of God. He also wants you to get into church where you will hear the Word and surround yourself with the right kind of people.

I know Christians who started coming to church, but because things didn't happen fast enough for them, they stopped coming, and now live lukewarm, blasé lives. This is how God feels about lukewarm Christians, "Because you are lukewarm, and neither cold nor hot, I will vomit you out of My mouth" (Rev. 3:16).

When lukewarm Christians start going through difficulties in their lives, they blame God or the church for letting them down, when in fact, the only people who let them down were themselves. It is up to every believer to get into the Word, study the Word, hear the Word, and learn who they are in Christ.

Some Christians believe the lie that it is too hard to study their Bible and go to church, let alone serve in the church. They believe it is just too hard to live for the Lord. When things don't get better, they tend to blame God or walk away from Him. According to the Bible, however, the way of the transgressor is what is hard. It is not hard living for God. What's hard is living for the enemy and having your marriage fall apart or your kids in jail. What's hard is living with addictions or going through rehab. What's hard is having the police knock on your door at two o'clock in the morning. In contrast to these realities, living for God is not hard; it is blessed with peace.

Undeserved Favor

Paul tells us in 2 Corinthians 5 that Jesus' blood has reconciled us to God. In other words, when I gave my life to Him, I was washed in the blood of Jesus. At that moment, I became the righteousness of God. I am right before God. God doesn't love me because I'm good. God doesn't love me because of who I am. He loves me because of who He is. Now that I have given my life to the Lord, nothing can ever separate me from His love—not devils, or angels, or anything I do, good or bad (see Rom. 8:39.)

> *Grace is the power of God to meet my need whether I deserve it or not.*

We define grace as God's undeserved favor. Grace is the power of God to meet my need whether I deserve it or not.

I don't have to earn grace. Grace comes to those who love the Lord. Our spiritual enemy tries to trick us into trying to earn our salvation. He is always trying to make us believe that God is mad at us. He wants to make us afraid of God, but the Bible tells us plainly that if we repent of our sins, God will forgive us. If we are willing and obedient, He will bless us.

God blesses His people because of what Jesus has done, not because of what we have done. In fact, it was Isaiah who said, "All our righteousnesses are like filthy rags" (Is. 64:6b). We can never be good enough, but the blood of Jesus covers our life so that all God sees is His own righteousness. We did not and cannot earn it, but when we called on the Lord, His righteousness covered us from the top of our head to the soles of our feet. It is not because we deserve it; that's why it is called grace.

Ultimately, you must learn that God blesses His people because of what Jesus has done, not because of what you do. If you're not careful, you will fall into legalism. You will fall into works rather than having a relationship with the Lord. Anyone who gets caught up in religious works will end up becoming frustrated and angry.

Anytime believers think that God is no longer close to them, they are in danger of trying to earn His favor back. We don't attend church to make God happy. Because we are His children, He is already happy with us. We attend church to grow. We don't serve in ministry or give our money trying to make an angry God happy; we serve and give because that's how we grow. We study the Word and come to church and serve in ministry so we can learn who we are in Christ.

The moment you begin to question why God isn't helping you, something in your mind is saying, "But you deserve to be blessed," or, "You don't deserve to be blessed." Either way, the Lord's blessings don't come to you as a result of you deserving it. God's grace and favor are not dictated by whether or not you have jumped through the right hoops. His mercies are new every morning because His love toward you is never-ending.

Resting in God

People become frustrated when they can't make the Bible "work" for them. They want to make the Bible say what they want it to say—as if they can control or manipulate the truth to fit what suits them. Instead, we need to get the Word of God in our hearts, speak it out of our mouths, obey what it says, and let the grace of God work in our lives by resting in Him (see Ps. 37:7). Sometimes we simply have to relax and say, "God, I'm going to trust in You."

If you are a frustrated believer today, you need to learn to relax and know that you are the righteousness of God, and let His grace work itself out in your life. When you know who you are in Christ, and that the grace of God is sufficient for you, then you will know in your heart that in due season God is going to work things out for your benefit (see Rom. 8:28).

When Paul talked about his need to repent from dead works, he wasn't just talking about sinful things. He was also talking about repentance from trying to earn favor with God. There is not one thing you can do to make yourself more righteous. The righteousness of God has nothing to do with you. You are righteous because He made you righteous through what Jesus did on the cross.

The Bible says, "In Him we live and move and have our being" (Acts 17:28a). Everything we need is tied up in Jesus. He makes us complete. When you connect your life with His, He will fix whatever is broken, heal whatever is hurting, and help you find whatever is lost. Wholeness comes not because of religion but because you are hooked up with the righteousness of God.

> ### *Wholeness comes not because of religion but because you are hooked up with the righteousness of God.*

When someone falls into sin it is usually because he or she is trying to meet some kind of a need. Falling into sin often results from an attempt to fulfill a legitimate need or desire in an inappropriate way; the desire to be loved, fulfilled, and happy. We will never experience complete fulfillment until we learn to rest in the Lord.

Looking at ourselves in the natural can make us become fearful. We can feel incomplete, because, by ourselves, we are. However, we are not alone. While our feelings tell us one thing, God's Word tells us another. Our feelings may say, "I'm a failure," but the Word says, "We are more than conquerors through Him who loved us" (Rom. 8:37). But our feelings are very real. When our feelings don't agree with God's Word, we have to remind ourselves of who we are in Christ. We should never live by our feelings, but always by the Word of God.

Complete in Christ

According to Colossians 2:10, every believer must reach the point of saying, "I am complete in Him." We must come to the place where we believe that Christ is all we need and ever will need. Say to yourself, "I am complete in Jesus." Repeat that simple phrase to yourself throughout the day. You will begin to feel His peace and strength rise up within you, replacing your fears and doubts.

When you don't keep the Word in your heart by meditating on it day and night (see Ps. 1:2), you will begin to question it. You will begin trying to find happiness outside of Jesus Christ. Once Satan succeeded in getting Adam and Eve to question God's Word, it was easy to get them to fail. The same thing is true today, once we question or depart from confidence in God's word, failure is not far behind.

Two great lies of the New Age Movement have to do with reincarnation and our so-called "godhood." These are the same two lies that Satan told Adam and Even in the Garden of Eden - you won't die, and you will be like God yourself. Countering lies such as these is why it is so important for us to stay firmly grounded in the Word of God.

What does the Word say about you? Satan doesn't need for you to deny Jesus in order to destroy you. All he has to do is to get you to believe that Jesus is not enough. His plan is to get you to question God's Word. Why didn't the children of Israel go into the Promised Land? After all, God had made them a promise. He said, "You're going to go into the land and defeat giants" (see Num. 14:8-9), and, "I'm going to give it all to you" (see Num. 14:24.)

The Israelites, however, said, "Oh, we're just grasshoppers next to the people on this land". We can't go up against them. Surely, God didn't mean what He said" (see Num. 13:33-14:3). In other words, they believed a lie. They didn't believe what God said. If God has given you a promise over your children, stand on that promise. If He has given you a promise over your finances, stand on that promise. Otherwise, you will never see it come to pass.

Faith and Obedience

The first Adam lost the authority that God had given him because he didn't believe, and therefore didn't obey. He fell victim to his own lack of knowledge, which resulted in lack of faith. Without knowledge, neither faith nor obedience are possible.

But Jesus, the second Adam, came to give us back the authority the first Adam lost. In order to receive it, we must have faith in God's plan of redemption and be willing to obey Him. We have to be willing to walk in love. The genuineness of our love will be proven in our faith and obedience. Will we love the Lord with our whole heart? Will we choose to love our neighbors as ourselves? Will we receive God's grace and forgiveness by accepting and loving ourselves? As I have quoted before, if we are disobedient and have hate or contempt for others in our hearts, we are not children of God (see 1 Jn. 4:20).

When we accept the work of God's love, when we receive the love of Christ into our hearts, we receive the abundant life He promised. He came to give us "exceedingly abundantly above all that we ask or think" (Eph. 3:20a). Down through the ages, the enemy has tried to convince us that we are not who God says we are, and that because we are not who God says we are, we cannot have what He says we can have. These are lies, pure and simple.

However, the grass withers and the flower fades, but the Word of God shall stand forever (see Is. 40:8). Go back to the Word. God and His Word are one. If there is anything you can count on or be sure of, it is God's Word to us in the Bible.

Freedom

Before we gave our lives to Jesus Christ, we were slaves—to sin, to our tempers, to our desires, to our flesh. But in Christ we are no longer slaves. We are heirs according to the promise of God (see Gal. 3:29.) Once you know that you are a king and a priest (see Rev. 1:6), you will have no problem saying "no" to drugs, because kings and priests don't do drugs; they don't engage in self-destructive behaviors because of low self-esteem.

Once you know that you are part of a royal priesthood, a member of the royal family, you won't be held captive to sin.

Once you know that you are part of a royal priesthood, a member of the royal family, you won't be held captive to sin. Because you've been adopted into the family of God, you're not a slave any longer. Because you are a child of the Most High God, you don't have to prove your identity. You don't have to earn your inheritance. My sons don't have to prove to me who they are. I know who they are. My sons are in my will simply because they are my sons. They know that whatever is mine is theirs, because that is part of their inheritance.

You are a co-heir with Christ, not a grasshopper. You have the right to walk in the blessings of God. You are a joint heir with Jesus. A son has hope for the future. A son knows he has an inheritance.

You've got to know who you are. You must know that God, the Father, wants to bless you. Now that you are a son and an heir, you can't let fear control you. Your best days are still ahead, and what belongs to Jesus belongs to you. Because He lives, you can face tomorrow. Because He lives, all fear is gone, for your God has not given you "a spirit of fear, but of power and of love and of a sound mind" (2 Tim. 1:7).

Even if you are facing something today that seems insurmountable, you need to hear the voice of the Father saying, "I love you. I've got a better life for you." The prodigal son was living in the pigpen, but he came to his senses. He decided to come home, and his father was waiting at the door with His arms open saying, "Come on, son. Come on home." Nobody ever loved us like Jesus.

LOVE MATTERS

CHAPTER FIFTEEN

It's a Love Test

If someone says, "I love God," and hates his brother, he is a liar; for he who does not love his brother whom he has seen, how can he love God whom he has not seen? And this commandment we have from Him: that he who loves God must love his brother also.

1 JOHN 4:20-21 NKJV

Life is a love test. When God Himself came to dwell among men, He showed us how to live our lives with love and grace. He demonstrated how we are to walk in love, and then, through the greatest love test of all time, laid down His life upon the Cross. Because of that one, momentous act of love, all of humanity can tap into the power of Christ to pass every love test with grace.

Unfortunately, many of us don't fully press into the Spirit, or dig deeply into the Word for instruction on the mechanics of operating in God's love. We think we know what walking in love is all about. We think we know how to love, and yet we are so fragile that if people don't treat us the way we want to be treated, we kick them to the curb. If they stumble, we talk negatively about them. If they are in need, we often look the other way. The point is, we don't know how to love with *God's* love, and that's why we must evaluate ourselves in light of truth—in the same light shed by the Spirit of Love.

As followers of Christ, we are all required to continuously develop our love walk in big and small ways every day.

The Love Journey

As both believers and disciples, we are on a love journey. First of all, as believers, we are continually learning more and more about the depth and infinite capacity of God's love for us. Secondly, as disciples, we are continually being tested and stretched to increase our own capacity to express that love anew in our daily lives. The more we learn, the more work we realize we must do. As followers of Christ, we are all required to continuously develop our love walk in big and small ways every day. If we tap into the power of Christ that dwells in each of us, we will not only succeed, but we will also experience more peace and joy than we ever thought possible.

Throughout the original Hebrew Scriptures, we witness epic love stories. In the Renewed Covenant, we are given the greatest love story of all time—the life and death of the Messiah. Not only are we taught how to love by the legacy Jesus left us, but the Spirit-inspired authors, Paul and Peter, James and John, also give specific instructions on how to apply in practical terms the lessons Jesus taught. They are all quick to drive home the point that without the knowledge of love, we are not children of God—in fact, we are nothing. Nowhere is this more eloquently or succinctly stated than in 1 Corinthians chapter thirteen. In this powerful "love chapter," Paul sums up just how important love is, how we are to recognize it, and, more importantly, how we are to demonstrate it. Concerning the latter, Paul wrote:

Love is patient, love is kind. It does not envy, it does not boast, it is not proud. It is not rude, it is not self-seeking, it is not easily angered, it keeps no record of wrongs. Love does not delight in evil but rejoices with the truth. It always protects, always trusts, always hopes, always perseveres. Love never fails.
1 Corinthians 13:4-8a NIV

Love is more important than anything else. Remember, Paul said that if we speak in a heavenly prayer language but don't know how to love people, we aren't doing anything but making a lot of noise. We may have all the gifts of the Spirit operating in our lives, but if we do not have love, we have nothing at all. Even giving away everything we own and sacrificing ourselves are meaningless unless they are motivated by love.

All the wealth, success, and notoriety in the world are worthless if we don't know how to love. No matter what you possess, what you do, or who you are, you will not have a satisfying or rewarding life without love. You can have butlers and maids, fame and power, but none of it will make you happy unless you have a solid understanding of the love of God.

The Simplicity of Love

There is nothing complicated about love. Love is not jealous or proud, but patient and kind. It's really pretty simple. Yet somehow we have come to think that jealous behavior is a form of love. Let me tell you, if you've ever met a jealous person, you know there is nothing kind about jealous people—they are mean-hearted. People who allow jealousy to operate in their lives have no understanding of God's love.

Of course, we are all prone to feelings of jealousy, but if we draw close to God, lean on the Holy Spirit, and develop an intimacy with the Lord Jesus, we will not be overcome by these emotions. Envy will not be able to take hold of us. We will be able to rise above pride, offense, and self-seeking. The power of God's love in our lives is that strong—but we have to do our part to renew our minds by spending time with Him and in His Word.

Love is a fruit of the Spirit, and we have to spend time in the presence of the Spirit if we want to bear spiritual fruit. In order for any of us to be fruitful spiritually, we've got to draw close to God. To have the fruit of the Spirit abounding in our lives, we must be in close relationship with Jesus. Because of this, it is easy to tell who spends time with the Lord and who doesn't. If you have a jealous streak, for example, it is because you are not close enough to the Lord that He can talk to you and deal with you about that issue in your life.

To have the fruit of the Spirit abounding in our lives, we must be in close relationship with Jesus.

Paul said that without love we are nothing. He might also have said that without love, we are afraid. The truth of the matter is that the jealous person is controlled by fear. Jealous people are afraid they are going to lose something that they think only one other person can give them. Envious people are afraid that if they don't have what someone else has, they will fail. They are compelled through fear to control or dis-empower others. They seek to manipulate others through their affection and attention, while it is they who are being manipulated by the spirit of fear. We know that such people are not led by the Spirit, because Paul tells us in 2 Timothy 1:7 that "God has not given us a spirit of fear, but of power and of love and of a sound mind." Jealousy is not rooted in love, but in fear, and it is a tool the enemy uses to keep us separated from God. Love and fear don't mix. It's that simple.

> ### *The reason the enemy doesn't want us to walk in love is because God's power works through love.*

Power Packing Love

The reason the enemy doesn't want us to walk in love is because God's power works through love. Galatians 5:6 tells us that faith works through love. If you don't know how to love people who have hurt you, then you will never know how to walk in faith. The Word of God urges us to "walk by faith, not by sight" (2 Cor. 5:7). Every believer knows that it is not easy to walk by faith and forgive the people who hurt us. But if we can't forgive people, we will never be able to walk by faith. Faith requires that we walk in love, and walking in love takes faith. Faith and love go hand-in-hand.

If we are going to develop the faith we need to overcome our enemies, we must learn to walk in love. Practically speaking, if we are to have power over anything, including our spiritual enemy, we will have to start loving people. This means forgiving them, which means not talking negatively about them behind their backs. We will have to forgive folks we don't want to forgive, and speak nicely about those who offend us. We can't rebuke the enemy on one hand and then talk badly about our coworkers on the other. If we don't walk in love, our faith won't operate.

As difficult as that may seem, if we understand that godly love is not a feeling but a choice, it becomes easier to choose love. When two people meet and fall in love, it's all about the feelings provoked by infatuation—what they see on the outside—feelings that have nothing to do with really knowing that person. It's an artificial love. The bottom line is, walking in God's love is a decision, a matter of deliberate choice. If you want healing to take place in any part of your life, you must choose to walk in love or your faith won't operate for that healing. If you need deliverance from your past, you must choose love at every turn.

Go to the Source

Growing the fruit of love in your life begins by drawing closer to God. The enemy knows that if he can keep you busy, distracted, and relying on your own strength, you won't find the source of power you need to walk in love. One of the enemy's greatest weapons against Christians is the snare of offense. Sometimes we become so offended we can't even consider taking time to seek God, let alone rest in the knowledge of Him. We get so bent out of shape that we take matters into our own hands. That's why offense is such a dangerous trap.

We all get hurt from time to time, but the test comes in how we choose to deal with it. Do we let hurts take root inside of us, or do we let them roll off? Do we allow bitterness to swell in our heart, or can we let it go without another thought? If we love the Lord, we are going to have to make up our minds to quit letting things that hurt us get inside our heart. As Scripture commands us, "Keep vigilant watch over your heart; that's where life starts" (Prov. 4:23 THE MESSAGE). This is a daily battle that requires that we learn to walk by faith and not by sight. At the same time that faith is a test of our love, love is a test of our faith.

Instruments of Love

God created us to be instruments of love and to bring healing to those around us. If we allow the enemy to succeed in getting us offended, then he will keep us from walking in love, and from fulfilling our potential as ambassadors of Christ—not to mention keeping us from the answers to our prayers. If we become offended by a person, an organization, or even society in general, the truth of the matter is that at that moment, we fail the love test. Remember that every opportunity to get offended is a love test! Passing or failing it is our choice!

The Bible says, "Do not give the devil an opportunity" (Eph. 4:27 NASB). What does that mean? It means that when an offense tries to come against you—and it will—you must not allow it to come. Some things you won't ever understand. You'll have to put them on a shelf and say, "God, I don't understand this. But I trust that You are working all things out for my good, and I know that my best defense is not to take offense! One day, Father God, you will show me what this is all about!"

To be the instrument of love God created you to be, you will have to learn how to avoid the snare—or trap—of offense. You'll have to learn how to steer clear of all the traps the enemy sets for you. He stalks all around just looking for those he can trip up with the pitfalls of pride, self-justification, and even self-righteousness (see 1 Pet. 5:8). Your best defense against the enemy's deceitfulness is learning to walk in love.

Your best defense against the enemy's deceitfulness is learning to walk in love.

Allow God's love to be perfected in you. Draw close to Him and spend time studying God's Word of love. Soon, those things that used to bother you will roll right off and you will wonder what the big deal was. While others continue to stumble along, you will walk over those rough places with ease, and discover how fit you have become for the Master's use. He will equip and empower you to pass every love test!

Other Books by DENNIS LEONARD

What Men Need to Know About Women
ISBN 1-880809-51-6

Happiness Mattters
ISBN 1-880809-63-X

Understanding the Baptism of the Holy Spirit
ISBN 1-880809-62-1

Your Best Days Are Still Ahead
ISBN 1-880809-53-2

Tus Mejores Dias aun Estan Por Llegar
[Spanish -Your Best Days Are Still Ahead]
ISBN 1-880809-55-9

Failure is Not the End, Revised & Expanded
ISBN 1-880809-43-5

Don't Judge My Future by My Past
ISBN 1-880809-15-X

Keys to Financial Freedom
ISBN 1-880809-20-6

About the Author

DENNIS LEONARD is an accomplished author, the CEO and founder of Legacy Publishers International, and has produced 2 gospel albums under his label Praizia Music. He is also the founder of Dennis Leonard Ministries and the senior pastor/founder of Heritage Christian Center in Denver, Colorado. Heritage is recognized as one of the most successful as well as most ethnically diverse churches in America, with more than 12,000 people in weekly attendance.

DENNIS LEONARD has been described by his peers—and the greater secular and spiritual community—as a true leader and an example to follow in the ministry of reconciliation between cultures and denominations. In September 1999, he was consecrated as Bishop of Multi-Cultural Ministries in the Full Gospel Baptist Church Fellowship. He is the first white man to be consecrated as a bishop with the Full Gospel Baptist Church Fellowship headed by International Presiding Bishop, Bishop Paul S. Morton, Sr. Dennis is also a visionary and answers the call of missions both overseas and here in the United States.